Praise for Don't Postpone Joy

This book will change the way you understand joy. Through the window of real stories, Mary Farr invites us to walk together on the 'holy ground of shared experience.' *Don't Postpone Joy* is far more than a self-help manual. It is a personal, poetic guide to embrace our human journey as a pathway toward personal transformation in the most ordinary of circumstances: festive meals, devastating losses, laughter, loneliness, creative risk, and the resilient longing for human fulfillment.

John Heagle, Catholic priest, counselor, writer, peace activist, and author of Justice Rising: The Emerging Biblical Vision

Don't Postpone Joy is more than a series of wonderfully engaging stories about faith, hope, and courage. It's a source of inspiration to help you navigate the uncertainty of the times we're living in. Mary combines her experience as a chaplain and educator with wit and compassion to deliver an uplifting read. No matter where you are in your journey to understanding how you fit into this crazy world, you'll find a relatable and caring guide in Mary through this lovely book.

Jennifer Havice, Growth marketer and messaging strategist at Make Mention

This book will inspire you and assist you in finding lasting joy in your own life. The stories are engaging and provide very good reading. I am sure it will be helpful and well received by many.

Fred Krehbiel, former CEO and Chairman of a Fortune 500 Company

Don't Postpone Joy is a jewel of a book. Mary Farr fills it with thought-provoking stories filled with wisdom, hope, and joy. This is a book filled with universal truths and themes that speak to all ages, no matter where we are on our life journeys.

Elizabeth Gold, former health care medical technology professional

Mary has an exceptional ability to connect readers with self and nature. *Don't Postpone Joy* is an amazing piece of work. It reveals Mary sharing her full self, authentic, vulnerable and funny. Her gift lies in an ability to tell a story and bring a reader to the exact place she describes. I am there and my senses are awakened. A thoughtful writer who strives to "listen to her life speak." She shares this wisdom, sorrow, and celebration with her audience. This book will touch your heart, inspire you, and give you hope.

Mary Christensen, Founder and President, Lync3 Health Care Leadership Development

Don't Postpone Joy offers a pathway to uplifting our lives from the world of chaos that seems to have engulfed us. After what seemed like a year of winter, struggling with Covid isolation and endless political meanness, Mary brings us a new book about rediscovering joy in our lives. She points out that it already surrounds us, and we just need to see and appreciate it. Helping us help ourselves is what Mary does so well.

Tom Palesch,, Business executive and traveling student of American landscape

Don't Postpone Joy is a wonderful collection of stories meant to help us find purpose, meaning, and joy in everything we do, whether it's watching birds in flight, finding a sense of the holy after the loss of a child, or simply walking a dog on a snowy Minnesota morning. Rev. Mary weaves her years as a hospital chaplain and her deep love of creation into a powerful message of hope. I couldn't put this book down.

Rev. Deacon Cindy Hillger, St. Martins by the Lake Episcopal Church, Minnesota, Former Journalist, WCCO-TV, CBS Minneapolis, MN.

I'm feeling gifted: gifted with "time out" moments: with moments of sanity in a world dizzy with its own self-interest; with moments of peace and beauty in the natural world that surrounds us. *Don't Postpone Joy* is one of those rare books that people will return to for the moments it shares. It deserves to be everywhere for readers to pick up for the sheer joy of reading it.

Clement Birch, Gold Executive with Watkins 1868

I loved this book and look forward to sharing it with many of my friends. It's filled with love, compassion, lots of good humor, grace, gratitude and joy. Thank you!

Barbara Peterson, Career woman's fashion representative

Also by Mary Farr

The Heart of Health

If I Could Mend Your Heart

Never Say Neigh

The Promise in Plan B

DON'T POSTPONE JOY

DON'T POSTPONE JOY

By Mary Farr

Published 2021 by Shorehouse Books
Printed in the United States of America

ISBN-13: 978-1-7372746-0-5

Dedication:

To Fred

For his infinite generosity and joyful enthusiasm for life.

Contents

Introduction

Tell me a fact, and I'll learn
Tell me a truth, and I'll believe
But tell me a story, and it will live in my heart forever

—Native American proverb

Several years ago, my daughter and I fell in love with Chautauqua. The Chautauqua Institution, a 750-acre educational center in southwestern New York State, hosts some 7,500 visitors on any single day during an annual nine-week season. In addition to timely topics and exceptional speakers, Chautauqua summer schools offer a tantalizing array of courses in art, music, dance, theater, and more. While this is not a commercial for Chautauqua, it serves as a grounding from which this book emerged.

Upon our first arrival, we unpacked and set out to get a look at the neighborhood. This included everything from lakeside bocce games to spectacular gardens and woodsy walking paths. One might call it a

1

front-porch community. Everywhere we walked, we encountered families and friends playing cards, eating lunch, and simply hanging out together on the front porch. At one point during our little tour, we discovered an imposing rock nestled among some daylilies in front of an old Victorian inn. Engraved on the rock was a simple statement: "Don't Postpone Joy."

Suddenly moved by this message, I took a photo of it. Eventually, I even taught a Chautauqua course by the same name. Yet it was the sense of déjà vu upon first seeing the rock that captured my attention. The words felt familiar. Then, the next day I remembered a long-ago experience of visiting a patient in a hospital where I served as a chaplain. Having just learned that he faced a life-threatening lung cancer diagnosis, this fellow requested a chaplain visit. I took the call and found him sitting in a chair, reading. We talked. Well, truthfully, he talked. It was more of an interview, as he asked about my work and why I'd chosen chaplaincy as a vocation. He also told me about his work and how it was enormously rewarding and all-consuming. He described spending a great deal of time traveling and away from his family. Finally, after a lengthy pause, he added, "Whatever you do, don't postpone joy." It would not be the last time I heard this entreaty spoken by a patient.

Since the day when we discovered the beautiful garden rock, my daughter and I have returned to Chautauqua as often as we can. And on every visit, we check to see that the rock still holds court in the garden. It does! And I am pleased say that a photo of it graces the cover of this book. We have since learned that the rock was a gift from the homeowner's husband, a gift he gave to her shortly before he died. By all accounts, their marriage had been a joyful one. Not exotic or filled with extravagancies but generous and full of delight and wonder.

That first day at Chautauqua started me thinking about how often we get in our own way when it comes to joy. Sometimes it feels as if we've forgotten how to make simple fun or waste time wisely with a friend. How easy it is to get so lost in the hustle of what we call living that we lose sight of what a joyful life could look like. We fall into the insidious role of human doings rather than human beings.

Each of our personal journeys offers us many memorable and rewarding gifts. Yet these same journeys test us with obstacles, do-overs, hellos, and goodbyes. This book encompasses my lived experience of how a joyful life encompasses a range of events and passages that shape us through pleasure, achievements, doubt, and even loss. From setbacks to success, marriage to divorce, or illness to health, life encounters can shut us down or open us to a heartfelt transformation.

The notion of growing toward joy implies movement—a process rather than an event or series of high points and happy episodes. I believe that a life of enduring joy points to a way of living and seeing the world rather than a way of winning or mastering the world. Enlarging our experience of joy requires increased self-awareness and attentiveness to what matters most and least. What is most precious, and what can we release? Where do we get stuck? It invites us to step into what I call a life review. This inner process helps us move toward rewarding goals. It also helps us let go of tired, unsupportive ones. This kind of self-inventory inspires long-term fulfillment and wholehearted living.

Years of hospital chaplaincy—listening, affirming, and comforting patients and their loved ones—has taught me a great deal, especially about the language of loss and healing. What is helpful and generative in times of a tragedy? What is not? How do we shape a future when the present appears to be in shambles? How do we find our way back to hope following catastrophic events surrounding the COVID-19 pandemic and an eruption of social pain propelled by systemic racism? In fact, this book took shape during the many months in which we have been isolated at home, watching and wondering when the world will recover. Thus, readers will encounter occasional references to the surroundings in which we find ourselves.

Life is and no doubt will be different going forward. I invite readers to explore this window in time through a collection of stories. Not grandiose or heroic stories but true, universal tales that help shine a light on the road ahead. From setbacks to success, boredom to exhilaration, or illness to death, we each are living life stories. These stories can either shut us down or open our hearts to a new and worthy chapter.

I suggest that we begin our journey together by thinking about three separate, though related, words—happiness, pleasure, and joy. Happiness speaks to externally triggered feelings that often find their base in people, things, events, and accomplishments. Pleasure typically involves a momentary feeling that comes from some of the same external events as does happiness. These could include a great meal, a pleasurable trip, a promotion, or an achievement that brings one pleasure. Joy, while not excluding elements of happiness and pleasure, embodies a more nuanced picture. This view anticipates finding peace with who we are (our authentic selves), why we are (how we become this self), and how we are (how we choose to interpret our lives).

History shows us that we are a society that spends lots of energy and money seeking pleasure and avoiding pain. Unfortunately, this kind of seeking can also result in addiction to external experiences. Nothing is ever quite enough. One can be a pleasure-seeker, though not experience deep and abiding joy.

The US Census Bureau reports that a third of Americans show signs of clinical depression and anxiety. These and other mental conditions have become amplified during the pandemic. They also have contributed to the increased use of mind-body modalities, such as yoga, meditation, and tai chi—modalities that once were used almost exclusively for pain management. So what does joy look like in a culture struggling with anxiety and depression?

My aha moment regarding the meaning of joy wasn't exactly a moment. It has evolved over time, and I still have many questions. This stretch of time has included a mix of delightful and rewarding experiences. It also has featured a measurable degree of darkness. Looking back, I recall a friend saying to me at a particularly low moment, "How inconvenient it is that we live our lives forward yet understand them backward." Indeed. We don't typically view the dark parts as worthwhile moments.

Yet I've also come to understand that most of what we learn in life begins with a question or problem. Imagine the hurdles scientists and mathematicians face before landing on a new discovery. Space travel, education, medical research, including vaccines and treatments, and even sports achievements typically begin with obstacles and do-overs. Considering this scenario, one can make a case that negative experiences aren't always the enemy. They can and often do open our eyes to creative solutions, overdue changes, and even opportunities. We face barriers and losses over time. Then, with a growing sense of self-awareness and confidence, we find the skills and motivation to make course corrections.

Failed marriages, lost jobs, health setbacks, and crushing financial burdens—none of us gets out of this life unscathed. The question is, how do we incorporate all of this into a package from which we can extract joy on a sustained basis. I believe we must first approach this subject more holistically.

It helps to look at joy as a range of experiences and passages. These are the things that teach and shape us. Our task is to examine what they mean, come to peace with their impact, learn to coexist with the negatives, and build joy from the whole lot.

Chapter 1
Setting the Table

When you do things from your soul,

you feel a river moving in you, a joy.

—Rumi

Last summer, a friend and I shared a deeply moving experience that took place at an extraordinary location—a field of sunflowers.

Founded by Jim Denevan, "Outstanding in the Field" consists of a traveling farm tour and presentation about sustainable agriculture. The tour and lecture are followed by a delectable meal prepared by a local chef. These events typically take place at select farms throughout the country. Each consists of a single gathering in a farmer's field, accompanied by a food offering of grateful appreciation. Rather than source ingredients for an award-winning restaurant, they bring the restaurant to the source, a field with cattle and turkeys wandering freely. Wine, dinner, and conversation get served up family-style to a group of strangers who have learned a meaningful lesson in how to grow grains, fruits, and livestock in a sustainable, earth-friendly manner. The point of all this was to connect diners with the origins of their food, while celebrating the hands that feed them—the farmers, chefs, cheese makers, and growers of all kinds.

This unusual experience also proved to be a joyful salute to human connection. Nearly one hundred guests gathered at one table to share the most fundamental and universal human conversation—a meal. It was magical. And I believe this magic was no accident. Food-related beliefs appear in many wisdom and cultural traditions. Nutritionist Deborah Kesten, in her book, *Feeding the Body, Nourishing the Soul*, discovered that honoring food through thoughtful preparation and then partaking of it with depth and sincerity genuinely makes it sacred.

Many religious and cultural traditions offer a spiritual perspective that we have forgotten over the centuries. When we furnish food with such sacred understanding, it nourishes both body *and* spirit. When we appreciate food in this manner, we also contribute, in an essential way, to healing and wholeness. Sharing food with friends and family further serves as a joyful celebration of connection and faith.

For example, most religious and cultural traditions enjoy rituals that use food as a means of connecting to a deeper spiritual significance. Jewish dietary laws honor the sanctity of the life inherent in both animal- and plant-based food. Christians sustain their connection to Jesus Christ through the bread and wine of Holy

Communion. African Americans season their soul food with love as a way of celebrating community and friendships. Yogis eat, in part, to commune with food's life-giving qualities. Muslims honor food for its divine essence. Buddhists pursue enlightenment by bringing a meditative awareness. This list is a long one.

Ironically, though we retain a rich history of food as spiritual and social sustenance, nutritional science today still focuses largely on biology. Food is typically viewed as a collection of nutrients—fuel for the body that can be measured and broken down into proteins, fats, carbs, and minerals. And all this is calculated in calories. While nobody would deny the value of research and our diet, excessive focus on nutrition can conceal the satisfying qualities and sheer enjoyment of eating, particularly eating with others. Preparation and sharing food in a community setting is vastly different than surfing an electronic device while knocking back a pizza. Beyond nutritional and convenience aspects, shared food also plays an essential role in happiness and joy-filled experience of one another.

While food took center stage in this Outstanding in the Field celebration, our earth, her seasons and productivity, and her fragility played equally powerful roles in the evening. We witnessed genuine respect for livestock, wildflowers, birds of prey, and even wild turkeys that joined the celebration. It reminded me of growing up in western Wisconsin where, at an early age, my brother and I learned the value of protecting water fowl, pheasant, and trout streams. My mother and I spent summers tracking fireweed and purple vetch. With a bucket of water and a *Peterson* bird guide, we counted meadowlarks and sandhill cranes. We even kept records of birds' migration dates.

Outstanding in the Field captured my imagination, especially the long table. I've even had dreams about the table—shaking out a huge tablecloth, arranging flowers, and setting the places in preparation of welcoming guests. This same image ultimately set the table for a class I've taught and a website dedicated to the subject of joy and hospitality. While this might seem counterintuitive amid a pandemic and shattering social upheaval, I decided to take a chance. Frankly, I'm not sure there has ever been a more important time to examine our lives, our values, our relationships, and our capacity to heal. I'm convinced that this idea of "setting the table" makes a case for discovering and rediscovering authentic joy. Together.

The words of Pierre Teilhard de Chardin capture the essence of this journey toward joy: "We are not human beings having a spiritual experience. We are spiritual beings having a human experience."

So how does one describe a spiritual experience in the context of joy? The following statements offer readers a framework for life as a spiritual journey:

A belief in some intrinsic meaning or order to the universe

A faith that humanity and creation are inherently good

An understanding that the force hidden in creation is a loving, present, and active energy

A trust that this active energy behind creation could be called God or a higher power

A willingness to accept what is (not to be confused with grudging resignation or approval of evil)

A fundamental expectation of future good

An ability to find peace of mind in an imperfect, ambiguous world

Building on this framework, the following chapters will explore who we once were; who we are today; why self-awareness matters; how it shapes our decisions and the quality of our lives; and what we can hope for in the future.

The last point, hope, constitutes a spiritual element of well-being and being well. Hope provides purpose, direction, and a reason for being. I would add that hope encompasses an assured sense that one can transcend any present situation. It is an attitude toward life, not just an occasional feeling to which we turn when we need it. It is a disposition that says the future is an open one, and I can dare to believe it holds integrity; that future good can occur even in the face of a loss or unplanned change of direction. Hope engages our capacity to see ourselves in a larger landscape, one in which we can transcend a present situation, whatever that might be.

In every age and season, there are people who feel abandoned by life. In each of our lives there are moments when we feel cut off from hope and from love. Yet we are invited to live in the real world of human paradox, a place where we won't be saved from the human condition, but we can grow and flourish within it. We cannot fix every injustice. We cannot cure every disease or withdraw from life's pain.

11

We cannot always solve the questions that plague our hearts. Instead, we can and must live them. While we cannot ignore the tensions that life delivers from time to time, we can continue to choose to receive life as gift and seek joy as a worthy destination.

Chapter 2
Pay Attention to Your Beliefs

Nobody has a purpose that wasn't meant to be shared. No matter our age, resources, or situation in life, we gain a deeper perspective of that purpose by engaging in what I call a life review. This simple practice helps shine a light on our gifts, motives, and opportunities for growth. All it requires is some honest mental tidying, made possible when we pay close attention to our beliefs as well as our dreams. For example, how have our beliefs shaped us? Where did they come from? Some beliefs emerge from our cultural roots, while others pass through generations as traditional foods, careers, and even political choices.

Two fundamental questions arise when we to pay attention to our beliefs is: where did I learn this, and does it remain life-affirming and meaningful? Is it time to dust these off and rethink their value? Is it possible or even wise to adjust some of my beliefs? Would it enable me to share my abilities and purpose in more profound ways?

The kind of life review I'm speaking of expects careful internal listening—to your life choices, your opinions, and your heartfelt desires. However, listening is a learned discipline and takes serious practice. A fellow chaplain once said to me, following a particularly tense department meeting, "It's impossible to listen until we stop talking, and I hope that I've learned to never miss an opportunity to keep my mouth shut." This also applies to the art of listening to our lives speak.

In my experience, as we get better at listening to our own history, wisdom emerges from the silence. We listen to our choices. Where have I traveled, and where am I today? Where have I been stuck, and where could I hope to be tomorrow?

How easy it is to drift through life, making decisions based on the same beliefs that might once have been sustaining but may be no more. Clinging to worn-out traditions and getting fixated on certainties can deter rather than enhance our happiness and satisfaction with our choices. Yet change is as complicated as listening. Sometimes we find it's easier not to change our beliefs, routines, and habits, even if an adjustment promises to add new light on the road. Instead, we respond to the option of change with something like, "Thank you, but I prefer to maintain the status quo. I'm too old to learn how to host a Zoom meeting, even if it means seeing my grandchildren during social distancing and quarantine caused by a pandemic."

I prefer to think of a life review as a series of internal "housekeeping" tasks that ask questions: What do I believe about myself and my world? What am I willing to change to make life more rewarding? This likely includes additional considerations: What can I let go of, and what holds me back? How can I develop my gifts or what I describe as personal assets? And speaking of personal assets, these are the admirable qualities we each possess, such as patience, creativity, courage, and compassion. Though they might not appear in a résumé, it is these gifts that contribute immeasurably to a purposeful life experience.

Think about your dreams. It's easy to drift through life, paying little attention to them. One day, we're twenty-five and charging off to join the flow. The next, we're no spring chicken and are wondering what happened to all those years. We realize that time has moved forward, though we might not have done the same. Dreams change over time. I once dreamed of marrying a Montana rancher. My plan included owning at least one hundred American Quarter Horses, plenty of Hereford cattle, and a few dozen good broodmares. I'm still looking for that cowboy!

We achieve some dreams. Some we don't. That doesn't mean it's time to stop dreaming. Maybe you are reaching for a dream right now, or maybe you gave up years ago. It's even possible that some of your long-held beliefs got in the way. This prompts an equally important life-review question: Are there people, expectations, and relationships that make it difficult to pursue your dreams? Or is it possible to make reasonable adjustments that enable you to move forward toward a new dream?

Beyond the dream conversation, we need to name what matters most to us going forward, which is not the same as ignoring others' needs and goals. It's essential that we know what brings us the simplest joy and sense of accomplishment. Equally essential is recognizing when we are contributing the most or the least and how we could make adjustments that deliver more significant rewards.

Exploring your beliefs can produce as simple a change as altering Thanksgiving dinner. Rather than serve the exact meal you have served for decades, how about serving your nephew's fabulous grilled ribs instead of turkey? Or roasted sweet potatoes with orange zest instead of serving them whipped with marshmallow topping?

Observing our beliefs also can result in life-changing health decisions. For example, many of us who came of age in the sixties smoked cigarettes. Our college dorm rooms reeked from blue clouds of smoke, as did the local pubs, restaurants, and even planes. I'm sure that most of us considered smoking a fashion statement, not a health risk. We know differently today, and many have made a change.

Then there was the time my mother caused a brouhaha when she moved the Christmas tree from its traditional spot in the living room and placed it in the library. Years later, we were still listening to family members whine about the time Mom ruined Christmas by moving the tree. That same year, she also dared to serve whole-berry cranberry sauce at dinner instead of the jellied version. As for the tree, the problem was size. Each year my brother and father brought home a bigger tree until the branches nearly reached the fireplace. In short, Mom was trying to avoid burning the house down. It's also worth noting that our resistance to change also can result in missed opportunities to taste something new.

My own resistance to change came to light decades ago following my ordination in the Episcopal Church. It had been a difficult path, during a time when women's ordination evoked plenty of angst and resistance. A significant number of clergy and church members held resolutely to their entrenched ideas of women in ministry. After a couple of years of attempting to fit into the local clerical culture, I chose to pursue a ministry of hospital chaplaincy. This led to a move to Minnesota and, ultimately, to Children's Hospital in Saint Paul, where I remained for years. The move was prompted, in part, by a des˙ earn a master's degree in theology from Saint Catherine Univers. fine Catholic women's university in Saint Paul. At that point, developed either cold feet or, more likely, resistance to change.

A work colleague and good friend quietly listened to my daily excuses for not enrolling at St. Kate's. "It's too expensive," I complained. "I already have a job, and it will take me too long to get through the program." On and on it went until one morning my dear friend sat quietly listening to one more diatribe about why making a change and entering the graduate program made little sense. After a thoughtful silence, she simply said, "Mary, the time will pass anyway, so why not spend that time doing something that matters?"

Of course, she was right. Completing that theology degree has opened the door to unimaginable opportunities and experiences. It has fostered a level of creativity, writing, teaching, and faith-sharing that I never would have attained, had I remained stuck in the prickly ordination experience I left behind. So while I firmly believe we all have a purpose and assets worth sharing, I am also aware of the excuses we use to avoid this kind of self-examination.

We all bring our unique gifts to every day. We adapt. We pivot. We create. We forgive. We initiate our ideas. We bring these talents to our parenting and personal relationships. We use them to make good decisions and to rise to life's challenges.

Imagine the personal assets you can grow and share with our world today. Might this process also contribute to your life's meaning and joy? Could it even help mend the torn fabric of our communities and our country?

Chapter 3
The Doctor Who Healed with Silence

Rabbi Shimon, son of Rabban Gamliel,
said, "All my life I have been brought up
among the Sages, and I have found
nothing as good for the body as silence; it
is not study that is the essence but the
practice, and whoever is profuse of words
occasions sin."

—Pirkei Avot 1:17

Once, out of the blue, I received an invitation to write a speech for a popular political figure. The address was to be given at an elegant dinner, hosted by a local hospital foundation. The event honored a physician's many years of skillful service to his patients in the community. It was a particularly busy time at work, and I accepted the writing assignment with some hesitancy—at least until I placed the first phone call to a colleague of the honoree.

"He's the finest doctor I've ever known," the fellow internist reported. "He's the kind of role model every physician could and should use."

A second call to a family friend produced a comparable response: "His life gives meaning to qualities like humanness, patience, and compassion. He deals with humble people as if they were important people and communicates sincerely with everyone he touches. And he never limits himself in his relationships."

It was puzzling that each person with whom I spoke shared stories about the doctor's temperament, his gift for mentoring young physicians, and his engagement in social justice but very little about medicine.

Several more calls left me thinking I might not have a story— at least not a story that would interest a health care organization honoring one of its own. Not one of my interviews included any evidence of the doctor's clinical skills. While everyone spoke highly of him, their observations had less to do with his professional competence than with his character and commitment to listen to his patients. It became clear that his career had opened him to a dimension of spirit that everyone recognized as a healing gift, worthy of honor and respect.

Aside from his obvious kindness, this man inspired patients in ways that helped them be well. His faithfulness to serve the life and people around him also strengthened the life within him and within his family. Though everyone insisted that he was a gifted doctor, they further described him as highly invested in his patients' well-being and being well. It became clear that he never allowed the business of health care or complicated insurance issues to disrupt his call to serve others through medicine.

Years earlier, this physician had decided to let go of the typical clinical obsession with fascinating medical problems. Instead, he immersed himself in the daily routine of a healer. With empathy and awe, he attended to the souls of his patients as well as their bodies. He soon discovered that a person's spirit was not just a human potential but a human need. From where he stood, too much scientific objectivity could make someone blind to the whole picture of health and healing. Though expert clinical skills rewarded him with a respected practice, he never lost sight of who he was and what he wished to share with the world. This man had made a remarkable commitment to care for others, to seek wholeness, and to recognize the value and dignity of each person he touched.

At the award ceremony, several distinguished guests regaled the audience with glowing stories about the honoree, showering him with well-deserved accolades. One shared a story about calling him in the middle of the night, frightened because he was having chest pain. The doctor always answered his phone, whether he was on call or not. Another described showing up in his office without an appointment, concerned that he had broken his shoulder in falling off a ladder. Nobody was ever sent away from the doctor's office without being seen and evaluated.

Finally, the time for the presentation arrived. Everyone waited expectantly, perhaps wondering what extraordinary or heroic stories he might share about his career in medicine. Instead, the physician shyly approached the microphone to make his acceptance speech. It was brief, but, from his point of view, not brief enough.

"There is nothing that becomes a person more than silence," he began. "Silence is a safeguard for wisdom." Thus, with a simple and gracious thank-you, he returned to his seat to finish his dessert. If anybody was disappointed at his lack of ceremony, they never showed it. Everyone seemed to understand perfectly.

In a place of quiet wisdom, this fellow had developed an uncanny ability to hear, nourish, and strengthen people. He practiced a rare kind of medicine. His sensitive ear and hospitable heart clearly informed his clinical competence. He embraced a simplicity synonymous with humility—a word derived from the Latin *humus*, meaning earth. To be humble means to be in touch with the earth and all her inhabitants.

Without question, we live in times of uprooted traditions, unclear guidelines, and fears about protecting our health and the health of those we love. Too often, silence and listening get canceled out by shouting and doubting. Too much attention is focused on winning and too little on wisdom. Some say that cardiac bypass surgery is a metaphor for our culture, a culture that has bypassed the heart and forgotten how to listen from the level of the heart. In many ways, alienation and cynicism have wounded us. Nagging doubts about the future of our careers, politics, finances, and personal lives can erode confidence and hope. Yet within this ambiguous center of anxiety lies a fundamental truth—we must listen to and connect with our own hearts and one another. We must sustain not just ourselves and our own dreams but also the hopes and dreams of others and of the larger community. Our future rests in our capacity to listen to our lives and to one another. Whether we're health professionals or simply trying to find the path toward wholeness, we all gain life when we realize the healing power this honored physician brought to his work and life.

Each of us is on a personal journey that offers limitless possibilities for healing. Whether we teach school, care for children, or practice medicine, nobody and nothing can take away our choice of how we will respond to life's disruptive encounters. The physician faces a woman newly diagnosed with breast cancer. He steps down from his clinical pedestal, removes the curtain that protects his heart, and listens. A friend makes room in her busy day for another whose marriage has met limitation and failure head-on. She touches the friend's hand and knows. An alcoholic finds freedom in recovery. He feels welcomed and challenged by his new AA family and wholesome friendships. A nurse places a cool cloth on the forehead of a fifteen-year-old girl who has just miscarried her baby. Sometimes, a simple touch or quiet presence requires nothing more than silence to perform its healing work.

Author and educator Parker Palmer writes extensively about community, spirituality, and social change. In his book *Let Your Life Speak*, he implores readers with a potent request: "Before you tell your life what you intend to do with it, listen for what it intends to do with you. Before you tell your life what truths and values you have decided to live up to, let your life tell you what truths you embody and what values you represent." Given the unsettled times in which we find ourselves, I believe this entreaty also invites each of us to watch and listen.

My experience as a chaplain tells me that everyone wants to be heard. Everyone wants to be validated and to matter. Like the honored physician, when we listen from the level of our hearts, we offer the kind of hope that can hold greater power than prescriptions or words of advice. This kind of listening also lies at the heart of justice, love, and peace. Yet it requires silencing ourselves and creating an empty space in which others can feel safe with expressing their ideas, needs, and fears. Our need to listen is surpassed only by our need to connect and walk together on the holy ground of our human experience.

If the honored physician brought a single priceless quality to his medical practice, it was his gift of attentive silence, offered to each patient who walked through his office door. If hope holds the future of the world, the fruit of the physician's gift holds the possibility of a renewed humanity.

Chapter 4
The Silent Wave of Isolation and Loneliness

A sense of belonging can foster well-being—and being well. Belonging invites well-being—and being well.

Everyone wants to belong. Everyone *needs* to belong. We belong to families of countless shapes and sizes. We belong to churches, support groups, work groups, book clubs, and professional organizations. Most certainly, we all know what it feels like to belong. Or do we?

The evidence suggests we do not. The Centers for Disease Control and Prevention (CDC) reports that social isolation and loneliness has officially become a public health problem. The American Psychological Association (APA) warns that the loneliness epidemic now represents a threat to public health that exceeds that of obesity. One study cited by the APA found that having stronger and deeper social connections was associated with a 50 percent drop in the risk of early mortality. The Health Resources and Services Administration (HRSA) reports that loneliness and social isolation can be as damaging to health as smoking fifteen cigarettes a day. Health research, including Harvard University's nearly eighty-year study of happiness in adult life, has proved that embracing community helps us live longer and be happier. The science says that loneliness kills. So how did this happen?

Consider just a few changes in our social structure and important relationships that have occurred in recent years. Begin with dispersed families and fluctuating neighborhoods. Add to this the vanishing social clubs and VFWs and diminished church membership. And one can hardly ignore the influence of digital technology, including social media, virtual learning, and at-home employment, topped off by an isolating global pandemic. All this and more leave us with far fewer opportunities to connect face-to-face with one another. It also offers far more opportunities to isolate.

So how do we define loneliness—an obstacle to joy? Years of listening to others' stories tell me yes. I have watched isolation and loneliness pave the way to anxiety and depression. And it's not about how many friends we have but whether we feel emotionally or socially disconnected from others. This can occur whether we are married with a family or living alone. Plus, we don't always recognize it in others or even within ourselves. Loneliness can be confused with belligerent or unconventional behavior. Consider the elderly uncle who comes for Christmas dinner, drinks too much, and then grumbles about the food and unruly grandchildren. Even an ornery uncle might not recognize his changed behavior since his son's overdose and death five years ago. Further, we typically don't walk up to someone and tell him he behaves as if he is lonely. Speaking of ornery uncles, I am reminded of what happened when two young girls invaded the space of a grumpy old horseman named Bob Stall.

"Horse crazy," our parents called us. No piano lessons, no summer camp, no party dresses—at age twelve, my friend Robin and I thought of nothing but horses and all the adventures we could cook up with our horses, Koko and Sherry. This passion for everything horse furnished a backdrop for the arrival of a new neighbor.

My mother reported that a man with racehorses had moved in next door. Of course, I wasted no time getting to the phone to share this good news with Robin. The only thing more exciting for us than dressing up our own horses was the prospect of meeting someone who raced horses. In fact, I had already decided to become a jockey, so this would fit right into my training program. But first, I jumped into my new Tony Lama boots, strapped on a favorite Gene Autry belt, and trotted over to meet the new neighbor.

The sagging barn was a little disappointing. Daylight streamed through the unpainted boards. Pink hollyhocks poked between an empty corncrib and a crumbling cement silo. Holes near the barn's foundation hinted of rats—or worse. It certainly didn't look like Churchill Downs, but maybe he had a property-improvement plan. Suddenly, a voice shot out, "Get the hell off my property!" I wasted no time doing just that.

This was not going to be easy, but after discussing a plan with Robin, I decided to try a different approach. The next day, I waited until late in the afternoon, when the old man left the barn for home. Once his car rattled out the driveway, I slipped across the pasture and into the tumbledown building. Armed with my Labrador retriever, Sam, I crept into a small feed room that smelled of molasses and alfalfa. Two horses peered curiously from their box stalls. The place looked modest but tidy. A grooming box next to the stalls held brushes, hoof picks, and sweat scrapers. A stack of clean towels, buckets, saddle soap, and assorted veterinary products neatly lined the shelves. But harnesses, not saddles, hung on the wall. A picture on the wall read "Dan Patch" beneath it.

I didn't stay long but vowed to come back to spy on the activities and then report all the details to Robin. So the next day, armed with my mother's birding binoculars, I stole through the trees and hid under some small jack pines near the edge of his exercise track. Much to my surprise, I learned that he owned harness racing horses, not saddle horses—two fine-looking geldings, one a trotter and one a pacer. He worked each horse every day while I spied from a safe distance.

Eventually, he discovered me and bellowed that I had better beat it. *Now!* I hightailed it home but already had decided that Robin and I were going to wear the guy down. An old horseman, with his deeply lined face and powerful hands that held the reins almost daintily, was not going to get away from us. After watching this training routine for a couple of weeks, I worked up the courage to try something new.

This time, I saddled up Koko and rode over to his place. Surely he couldn't reach me with those huge hands if I stayed on the horse.

I watched and waited as he led the pacer up the drive in my direction. To my surprise, he just walked around us without a word. At the edge of the track, he adjusted the hobbles, checked the horse's blinkers, and climbed into the sulky. It was as if he didn't even see us standing in the path. Koko and I just eyed him silently as he walked away.

Watching the workout made my heart pound. I had no idea pacers moved at such speed. Dust swirled beneath the sulky wheels, and I could hear the harness slap against the horse's flanks. After completing the exercise session, Mr. Stall walked his winded horse twice around the track to cool him out. He then headed toward the driveway, where Koko and I waited nervously.

"What's yer name?" he grunted, climbing out of the sulky and releasing the harness overcheck.

"Mary," I replied, attempting to calm the tremble in my voice.

"Okay, Marian, if you're so blessed interested in what I do around here, climb off that old nag and cool this one out."

I cautiously slipped out of the saddle and tied Koko to a tree. Mr. Stall buckled a halter on the gelding and handed me the lead rope. From that day forward, he called me Marian. What began as a hair-raising exchange with a cranky horseman turned out to be an unexpected adventure. Soon, Robin and I would share his small world of oats, liniment, and horse-racing memories from years past. We learned about Dan Patch, a pacer who set a record for covering a quarter mile in one minute fifty-five seconds as a nine-year-old. The record lasted for thirty-two years. Old Bob talked about the great horse Hambletonian and the Hambletonian Stakes, a famous race that began at the New York State Fair in 1926.

Bob eventually agreed to shoe Koko. He taught us how to care for our horses' feet and how to give them a proper bath. He drove us to the Chippewa County Fairground harness racing stable to meet his only friend, George Ashe. The two of them talked about trading horses in Fort Dodge, Iowa, and winning races in Milwaukee. Robin and I sat on a tack trunk, listening to tales about runaways on the racetrack, overturned sulkies, and screaming fans.

At first, nobody believed that old Bob let the two of us come onto his property. He had a reputation for running people out of his barn and out of his life. We didn't know this. We had no understanding of the loneliness that had haunted him since his wife died in a car accident years earlier. All we knew was we couldn't get enough of his stories about grandstand calamities and racetrack speed records. As for his own geldings, he said they once had been great prospects at the track until one suffered from a life-threatening puncture wound to his chest by running into a metal fence post. The other horse shin-bucked during his early training, causing an injury of the cannon bone that ended his racing career. The puncture wound required months of care and ultimately left a jagged scar. In both cases, the geldings required more rehabilitation than their trainers chose to invest. That was when Bob agreed to take them home with him. I never learned whether he later raced them again or simply enjoyed their company.

Robin and I had stumbled into the world of an isolated old fellow. Life's losses had shut him down. His horses comprised his circle of friends. Old newspaper clippings provided his only social contact. Our unusual friendship eventually lured Bob into my mother's kitchen for coffee and to Robin's house to meet her Shetland pony, Midge. None of us would have labeled Bob's problem one of loneliness, yet our mutual love of horses offered a bright human connection for a solitary guy who finally said yes to letting someone into his life.

The amazing thing about loneliness is that it's preventable, and good personal relationships are indispensable. In most cases, averting loneliness doesn't even require medicine, professional care, or a big budget. We can reach out. We can call. We can visit. We can include others and invite multigenerational others to join our activities and get-togethers. We can initiate deeper, more meaningful conversations that help others feel seen and loved.

The loneliness epidemic is not going to go away but will continue to grow. We, in our local communities, can have a significant impact on healing and preventing loneliness. We can make it happen.

Chapter 5
Faith: It Grows on You

Now is the time. Now is the place. Now is the opportunity to trust ourselves to make a difference. Today is a new day. We can claim faith in ourselves and in our Creator by seizing the moment. Each of us possesses priceless abilities that might not show up on a résumé but that hold real healing power. Empathy, generosity, compassion, creativity, and, yes, faith—to name just a few. Each time we claim these assets, we release restorative energy within ourselves and within the community around us.

Faith, as I understand it, is an attempt to come to grips with the paradox of human life and the complicated world in which we live. Faith, at its core, is deeply rooted in the expectation of future good. It embodies a spiritual journey that stretches us beyond hope and lives at the level of the soul. While life can be harsh, a spiritual life based in faith enables us to face setbacks and losses yet trust that goodness lies ahead.

The word *spirit* comes from the Latin word *spiritus* and signifies breath or wind. It's basic to humankind, a vital element of our individual and collective humanity. Treatment professionals have long known that chemical dependency affects every part of a person, including that person's spirit. Thus, when someone begins to seek the fullness of living at a spiritual level, she also begins to recover from addiction. A spiritual awakening tends to help one see and feel things he could not see or feel before. A spiritual awakening opens the door to knowledge previously hidden. This is the place on the journey in which power shifts toward something larger than oneself, a source of wisdom that can guide us through loss, growth, and healing.

Why is there such unhappiness and suffering, such greed and exploitation in the world? What can we make of this unpredictable mix of people and harrowing events that we call life? What kind of world is this, and what role might faith and the spiritual life play in it? Is the world as good as we hope or as bad as we read on social media? Is there something that is ultimately valuable and worth preserving? Faith says yes. It does so by lighting the way through darkness and inspiring resilience and courage in times of weakness and despair.

A life of faith is just that—a life, not a single event but a series of breakdowns and breakthroughs, faith lost and faith recovered. The faith journey encompasses obstacles and backslides as well as healings and victories. This is no simple sojourn. It's a tour in learning to trust. The tour takes place within the disarray of human experience, not outside of it. Though solitude may be a fine friend of faith, isolation—or insulation—from the mainstream is no place to learn about it.

Humankind, it seems, engages in a perpetual spiritual quest. We try to make sense of what appears, on certain days, to be nonsense. We need to know that our lives mean something. We want to be counted as valuable and hope that somehow what we are and what we strive to be will make a difference. As we start to explore the question of Creator, or higher power, or God, we begin to see ourselves as having something of the image of this entity that I call God. We see a capacity for having some sort of dialogue with God. Through a spiritual evolution, we enter a kind of partnership with this creative source, who assures us of a hopeful future. This knowledge tells us that life indeed does have meaning.

We live in a time, however, when broken fellowship with one another and with the earth strikes at the root of much world order. Our sense of covenant with our neighbor, our earth, and our Creator dangles by a thread. Among friends and within communities, we sense a loss of or longing for connection. We long for wholeness—a renewed faith. In this year of conspiracy theories and terrorism, the whole world waits on tiptoe for the emergence of a higher form of courage.

Faith and courage originate in the same family. Without faith, courage loses its focus and direction. The only courage that can prevail, the higher courage, must be interwoven with faith so that it can effectively express itself. The choice of faith is available to each of us. When we say yes to the possibility of a higher power, we set out on a search that ultimately reveals life as a gift, rather than an obligation filled with punishing obstacles. When we say yes to the possibility of God, we begin to understand how we fit into this tapestry we call creation.

Before I moved to Minnesota, I lived in a charming old farmhouse perched on top of a western Wisconsin hillside. A sweeping vista of neighboring farms and meadows graced every window of the house. Through these spacious windows, we inspected each season as it unfolded before us, much as a painter inspects her oils taking shape on a clean canvas. One December morning, I sat at the kitchen table, writing and watching a winter storm close in around the house, just as it has this morning. A luxurious snowfall began to envelope the countryside. The chestnut stubble of cornfields slowly sank beneath a soft mantle of white. As the wet snow continued to fall, I could no longer distinguish a hilltop from a valley or a pasture from a roadway. Fences began to blend into the murky backdrop. Rivulets of slush streamed down the window, completely blocking my view and detaching me from any life or movement beyond the glass.

Nevertheless, though I could see virtually nothing, I knew what was happening outside. I knew there were Hereford cattle and a couple of horses probing the soft snow in search of the last morsels of alfalfa. I knew that a cluster of calves galloped about, tails kinked high in jubilant bewilderment at their first encounters with winter. I expected that the brisk wind would tug at the remaining oak leaves and tangles of bittersweet in the woods north of our colt pasture. Chances were that Molly, our pet border collie, was flinging herself into the gathering drifts, pursuing anything that was airborne. I felt confident that when the snow stopped falling, she and I would find some congenial chickadees in the lilac bushes, waiting for me to fill the feeders.

All this I knew as I know God, not through any educational process but through experience and faith. I had no visual evidence of what was going on outside, yet I understood because I have always lived in the upper Midwest. I've experienced the changing seasons; the mood, stimulated by a big snowfall; the temperament of pets and livestock. Similarly, we sense God or a higher power through experience, a presence, a breath of someone or something creative and infinitely good.

Yet for many, the concept of God is too difficult to take in. Science and a process of logical deduction have led us to believe that creation has already occurred, leaving no room for human contribution. This is only half true. Land, water, and vegetation may be complete, but we are the inheritors of all this creation and creativity that has evolved for billions of years. We are the perpetuators of this creation, and we are the stewards of its resources. We can accept or reject the invitation to preserve and propagate creation as a gift of great value.

If we feel we are an accident of creation or a biological slipup, we have no reason to think we will be anything other than what we've always been. If we believe in a Creator who cares about humankind and about creation, we see a future that holds unlimited promise and potential. God, the artist. God, the maker of life. God, who weeps and laughs, who cradles this fragile planet and her children, not in contempt but as one cradles a newborn infant. This kind of faith says that each of us is called to co-create with this God. It is at that point that we begin to see this unimaginable gift that affords us both dignity and responsibility.

Faith is inherently linked to creation, not a creation of the past or a single event or violent bang that produced the world as we know it. Creation is an ongoing, regenerative event. Creation is in us, and we are in it. Creation feeds us and teaches us about humility and divinity.

Faith, then, is the energy that pulls us from hesitation. It propels us toward discovery of our life purpose and secures us in the promise of a journey well spent. It doesn't enable us to leap off our dull or difficult course, but it does free us from cynicism and smallness of thought. Faith is an act of fundamentally trusting the ordinary and the everyday. It invites us to value the humanness of ourselves and our fellow wayfarers. Faith gives us the energy to embrace life as a gift we cannot earn or grasp, but one that waits to be received in openness and shared in love. Perhaps most of all, faith allows us to offer ourselves, plain or fancy, broken and incomplete, to the creative rebuilding process of each day.

Chapter 6
Looking for Meaning—Together

This story is a reflection on an encounter that took place twenty years ago. Two decades later, we have entered a new season, a season in which we are again called to examine our hearts, to learn, and to grow. Together.

One in creation, you and I
Kindred spirits
Beloved
And bound together
Untouched
By a world of limitations
Walking together
Upon the holy ground
Of our shared experience

Knowing

We are human

And

This is enough

The message asking me to come to Labor and Delivery arrived at about four in the afternoon, an hour before the shift change. The social worker had just interviewed the Morgan family and felt they might benefit from a pastoral presence. Though they did not belong to a local church, Mr. Morgan expressed curiosity about meeting a woman minister.

"Mom is nearly full term, and her baby has died," reported the social worker, highlighting some of the pertinent details in Mrs. Morgan's chart. "She also has three small children at home and probably suffers from serious psychiatric problems," she mumbled offhandedly. Maybe bipolar disorder, schizophrenia, or borderline personality—or any of several other harrowing possibilities. The woman's reaction to her baby's death seemed "flat," according to others present at the nursing station. Most of the staff agreed that Mrs. Morgan had been joking oddly and that she failed to grasp the meaning of what was taking place in her life and her body.

A discussion then ensued about Mrs. Morgan's intellectual competence. The staff had given her some printed material about grief and loss, though they couldn't tell if she understood any of it—or even cared, for that matter. Perhaps the loss of this child was a relief to her, given that she had a brood of very young children at home. The nurses and case managers continued to speculate about the situation. An unspoken question underscored their discussion: *Why would the Morgans continue to have children when Mrs. Morgan was so sick and already had three youngsters under the age of four?*

I too wondered about the entire incident as I observed the facial expressions around me. The expressions denoted everything from bewilderment to hostility and self-righteousness. "How about the baby's father?" I asked. "Is he here?"

He was.

According to the staff, Mr. Morgan was behaving strangely too. His strident voice and peculiar jokes made them uneasy. He dominated his wife, bossing her and hardly permitting her to answer questions for herself. Troubling too were his constant references to what he called his wife's "medical mismanagement." He clearly thought that this might have contributed to their baby's death, and his questions were having a chilling effect on the various health professionals engaged in his wife's care.

Yet although he was overbearing and odd, in other ways Mr. Morgan appeared supportive of his wife—quite sympathetic and reassuring. A strong bond clearly existed between them. As I listened to the cacophony of opinions about the couple, it struck me that they were just that—individual opinions reflecting individual preferences, experiences, and comfort levels. The final diagnosis: Mr. Morgan talked too much, and he was ... well, she was ... that is, they were different. The social worker nodded in agreement.

I soon discovered that the Morgans were, indeed, different. They differed from me and from the rest of the staff in ways that hindered much meaningful contact. While the differences began at a racial level, they included profound social, cultural, educational, and financial contrasts. The Morgans embodied what could be described as a subculture of loss. The rest of us—white, middle class, and educated—exemplified a culture of privilege beyond the Morgans' experience or even comprehension.

The term *privilege* does not automatically jump off my tongue when I describe myself. Neutral or benign, perhaps, in the face of those who are culturally different but not privileged. To my knowledge, I've never intentionally wielded power over others. Nothing in my upbringing or education gave me any training in seeing myself as an oppressor. In fact, social justice ranks high on my list of priorities, a core value that has shaped my vocational call. But I also know that I spend most of my working moments in the company of other whites, a relatively easy audience for me to identify and negotiate with. Rarely do I experience obstacles or setbacks that I can't transcend with a little determination and courage. In addition, I possess a convenient little bundle of provisions, tools that make my life uncommonly palatable— a passport, checkbook, credit cards, a home, a car that runs, health insurance, and, perhaps most significant, choices. This kind of privilege has little to do with my good intentions. A lifetime of good intentions did not make me any less privileged in the eyes of the people I was about to meet.

Mr. Morgan greeted me loudly, with a predictable remark about never before having met a lady preacher. A thin veneer of jolly chatter barely concealed his anxiety and confusion. It wasn't long before he got to the point of his concern. "They say that our baby be dead for a long time," he announced, "maybe a month. Maybe it plans on risin' up like Lazarus! Do you think so, Reverend?" He slapped his knee and, with a loud guffaw, beckoned to his wife, evidently granting her permission to chuckle with him over his ice-breaking joke.

She lay quietly in the bed, staring out the window, uncommitted to a discussion of any type. Mr. Morgan veered from one unrelated topic to another, regaling me with stories about everything from his tour of duty in the US Army to the theology of Martin Luther.

I asked if they had friends I could call for them.

"No," he replied. "We keep pretty much to ourselves. I maybe leave the house to go to the grocery store, but I don't stay away long. We stick with each other and our kids most the time."

"How about family?" I pressed, hoping to identify someone who might lend support.

Mr. Morgan's parents had died some time ago. Mrs. Morgan's mother lived in Arkansas but didn't have a telephone—or much else, for that matter. Neither of them knew how to reach any other relatives.

"No, we don't need to call no family," said Mr. Morgan. "We can take care of this ourselves."

Soon, I learned that the Morgans had left Arkansas six months earlier. They were heading for Canada when their dilapidated car broke down on the freeway. A highway patrolman arrived and, upon discovering that they had no automobile insurance, collected a $300 fine from them. The encounter left the family broke and marooned in the Twin Cities. When we met, they had already moved several times in search of a safe neighborhood for their children.

"A baby always loves you, you know. Like, I know that a baby needs me to take care of it. I like that, don't you? I'm scared," Mrs. Morgan whispered.

"A lady preacher. Well, now, ain't that something? It would be good if you stayed with my wife while she has that baby. You know, my sister lost a baby once. And my wife's mama lost twins. Hell, we've lost a lot of children, now that I think about it. Yes, you could be a comfort to her when she has that baby."

Loss of power. Loss of identity. Loss of life.

"Is there anyone you would like to see or anything I could do for you?" I asked. "I've never had a child die. I don't know what it's like to be who you are or where you are. I'm sorry."

"That baby ain't never done nothin' wrong, has it? God is gonna welcome that baby, isn't he? 'Course he will. I know it couldn't be no other way. I mean, what's that baby ever done wrong anyhow? 'Course God is gonna do that."

Loss of dignity. Loss of hope. Loss of dreams.

"You know, the other day I come out to get in the car, and the horn started to honk. Just like that. It was the day my wife found out that the baby died. That darn horn be honkin' all the way downtown. People kep' lookin' at me, and I kep' holdin' my hands up in the air— like this—so they could see I wasn't doin' it myself. It was goin' itself.

Craziest thing I ever did see. I think maybe that baby's spirit was right in that car, don't you know? That be it. I know it. That baby's spirit was right in that car, tellin' us it was gonna be just fine up there in heaven. Do you think so, Reverend?"

Loss of access. Loss of privacy. Loss of connection.

"Mr. Morgan, I was wondering if the three of us could hold hands for a few minutes."

He struggled out of his chair and made his way to the bedside, where he took his wife's hand and then mine. We stood motionless against a backdrop of fetal monitors and rush-hour traffic.

Gripped by my own inadequacy, I offered a halting prayer of encouragement—for all of us. Tears slowly slipped down Mr. Morgan's cheeks. Mrs. Morgan kept her silent vigil, seemingly trying to summon the courage to give birth to her dead child.

We tightened our grips on one another's hands, a spontaneous gesture that found me at once understanding everything and nothing.

It was but a mere hesitation, a suspended moment in space, when we three said *yes* to a life briefly shared and broken. Wordlessly, we acknowledged the fragile and precious thread that knitted us together, suspended in time and creation. It felt like a merging of kindred spirits, never to be separated by a world of human limitations.

Chapter 7
Making Peace with Doubt

A month or so after New York City endured the blow of aircraft breaking her heart, I heard an intriguing story on National Public Radio. The journalist who authored the story had been in Brooklyn on that fateful day of September 11, when he happened upon a neighborhood park. It was shortly after the first plane struck the World Trade Center. People had congregated in the park to gaze in disbelief at the smoldering skyline. Clutched in twos and threes, they hunkered around portable radios, incredulous over the emerging details of what they were witnessing. With morning coffee in their cups and leashed dogs straining to meet their canine neighbors, the observers struggled to grasp the meaning of the horrific sight.

After observing the worried who had been gathering for some time, the journalist noticed a single individual at the far edge of the park. Unlike the others, this man had no coffee or family pet at his side, only a set of golf clubs and a large basket of balls. With a seven iron in hand, he methodically placed one ball after another in front of him. After carefully arranging his feet and correcting his grip, he hit each ball out of the park and into tall grass on the other side of the street. He gave no indication that he would be retrieving the balls. Nor did he look up at the fiery skyline crumbling before him. The journalist watched with curiosity, trying to understand the man's apparent indifference to the mounting catastrophe. Torn between his desire to learn the answer and his unease at interrupting a stranger's privacy, he finally got out of his car and approached the golfer.

"Good morning, sir. Excuse me, but do you know what has taken place at the World Trade Center?" the journalist queried cautiously. Silence. "Do you often come here to practice your swing?" he persisted. Again, he got no response.

After a lengthy silence, the golfer looked up, not at the skyline but at the stranger addressing him. "Yes, I do know what has taken place," he replied. Then he drove another ball into the rough grass. "I know what I've heard. I don't understand it, and I can't do anything about it." He resumed his practice. "But I can hit these golf balls."

After a reflective pause, the journalist finally replied, "You and I might not understand, nor can we control what's going on around us, but we do understand some things and can trust they will be there when this is over. Even in fear and doubt, we can uphold those golden elements of life that endure."

The Episcopal Church's *Book of Common Prayer* includes a Eucharistic prayer that speaks to the enduring beauty of something we all can grasp—our natural world: "At your command all things came to be: the vast expanse of interstellar space, galaxies, and suns, the planets in their courses, and this fragile earth, our island home." It is this fragile earth and her equally fragile guests that face persistent questions about brokenness and truths of the human condition.

As I write this, it's October 2020, nearly Halloween. Ancient mythology marks this as the beginning of the sacred season, when the gods came close and walked upon the earth. This October, we face a different kind of visitor, a black cloud of civil turmoil and life-threatening disease. The air is thick with anger and pain. Can we honestly believe in future good? Can we truthfully examine our attitude toward compassion, justice, and forgiveness? Do we look forward to the healing of our country or more of the same chaos? Is it safe for us to anticipate, with some degree of optimism, that the future will endure and is worth embracing and protecting?

I have no way of knowing whether the golfer in the NPR story moved into a current of hope. I suspect these first manageable steps with his golf club helped him secure some order to the chaotic events of the day. At least he could manage a bucket of golf balls. Hopefully, he had someone to talk with and to help him move toward healing. My guess is that in the year 2020 (and forward), most of us have looked doubt in the eye and wondered what is valuable in life. In what can we place our trust?

In the Hebrew Bible, the book of Ecclesiastes is called *Qoheleth*, and it was this wisdom figure, Qoheleth, whose purpose was not so much to teach about God but to tell what he had discovered about life—what humans might gain from life. He sets forth certain and seemingly cynical viewpoints on the value of life. He outlines a doctrine of opposites, like two currents flowing between the same banks. Woven into the pessimistic fabric of his composition, Qoheleth asks a larger question about the worth of life. What real value does life have to offer? How do we come to grips with the mystery and darkness of events we can't fix but can only experience? These questions and their accompanying angst have persisted throughout human history.

That September 11 morning, they likely troubled the golfer and the clutch of neighbors who watched the World Trade Center fall into ruins. Realistically, most of us will face a significant event in our journeys that has or will prompt questions about the future. And we don't need to witness the shattering of a city to slip into that same field of doubt.

We live in a world that longs for new resurrection. We long for it in our society, our communities, and throughout the world. When people ask me, "Where is God, or what is God's role in today's world?" my answer can only be that the God I know is right here. The faith that I understand does not consist of a belief that we will be rescued from life. It consists of a belief that we are loved. We are called to share that love with one another.

Soon, we will celebrate Thanksgiving, albeit this year's celebration will be smaller and quieter than most. Usually, when we talk about celebration, we think of festive events, such as weddings, reunions, and holidays like Thanksgiving. We remember times when we could forget, for a while, the hardships of life and immerse ourselves in an atmosphere of music and laughter. And this is invaluable.

But celebration, in a spiritual sense, moves beyond this. It is possible only through the deep realization that life and death are never found separate from one another. This kind of celebration can come about only when doubt and faith, joy and sorrow, weeping and laughter, birth and death—all those opposites—can coexist without overwhelming us. This kind of celebration accepts life as fundamentally good and precious. And our lives together are good and precious.

I heard the golfer's story in 2001, on my way back to Saint Paul from my Wisconsin childhood home. Driving along that late afternoon, the view from my car window felt comforting and familiar. I trust that autumn, with its clear skies, radiant maples, and shimmering red oaks, will continue to show up on schedule every year. The fields stand naked of their grains. Farm tractors bump over the country roads, hauling corn, soybeans, and hay to their winter storage spaces. The rural landscape rests quietly, waiting for the leaves to complete their cycle and become host to winter's softness.

Autumn marks nature's last hurrah. It's a reliable fact. Yet shorter days and cooler temperatures also stir in us a sense of sadness. Just on the other side of color and clarity hides an edge of sorrow. We must say goodbye to summer. This year, it also stirs a sense of loss and confusion about the future. If autumn reveals the persistent human questions concerning our search for that which endures, winter calls us to listen to God's reply.

In our quest for lasting things of value, faith in human goodness offers many possibilities, especially our capacity to heal and to care for one another. Yet faith in our humanity does not remake the human condition, nor does it undo human cruelty or disregard for life. Faith, like its partner, hope, does not reshape the natural forces around us. Whether we believe in a God or not, time continues to flow. Nature remembers to move through her cycles. Faith changes nothing in the external world of fact but transforms everything in the inner world of the spirit. It enables us to see our lives within a larger landscape—connected to all others. Faith gives us life viewed from the vantage point of love.

Chapter 8
Surprised by a Diary

When happiness eludes us—as eventually it
always will—we have an opportunity to examine
our programed responses and to exercise our
power to choose again.

—Father Richard Rohr

My mother, a child of two vaudeville entertainers, began her life on a definitively sad note. Her parents abandoned her so that they might travel the country unencumbered by an infant daughter. In fact, they left her in an orphanage, where she remained until a good-hearted aunt and uncle adopted her. By all accounts her adoptive family provided a safe and stable home, though she described her childhood as a very lonely one. Years later, eager to start a family of her own, she married my father and soon became pregnant with their first child. However, this too seemed ill-fated, as the baby boy died during a traumatic birth that led to my mother's long and painful recovery.

After a series of life-altering losses, she now faced one that could easily have left her mired in sorrow. She might have chosen to give up, to stop trying to find her way to happiness. She could have simply said no to a life that seemed to hand her nothing but heartbreak. Yet this is not how the story ended. Instead, she took the opportunity to exercise her power to choose again. That's when my mother learned how to cook. She also discovered her ability to create hospitality. She instinctively knew how to fashion space in which friends felt safe, welcomed, and well fed. Doors closed for her, yet the rest of the world opened to a new day. This was a truth I was about to discover in her diaries.

A recent fall nesting impulse found me mining beef stew recipes and sifting through an old Victorian secretary that sat in my living room. The secretary, chock-full of my mother's personal correspondence, had stood undisturbed for several years following her death. Perhaps this was my way of preserving my memory of her. Yet on this day, I felt moved to investigate the contents and, in doing so, made a surprising discovery—a diary. Interesting that nowhere in this diary did I unearth any revelations of old romances, or a mother's commentary on my brother and me, or even her cherished trip to Greece. This diary spoke of nothing but food, hospitality, and the joy of feeding her family and friends.

My big surprise turned into an afternoon immersed in an unsuspected piece of family history. It also revealed a road map to the many layers of nourishment that reach beyond nutrition. It all started with an introduction to my mother's sous-chef.

> *Page 1*
> Beef roast from Med [short for her butcher, Medwin]; 20 minutes per pound, begin in cold oven turned to 325 degrees.

This small entry sparked a memory of her frequent phone calls to Med requesting something special from his cooler. Her choice typically prompted his instructions for preparing a beef-roast beauty or plump leg of lamb. Med operated a tiny market called Obert's Grocery, located a few blocks from our home. It might not have passed today's public health department inspections, but anyone who knew her way around a kitchen knew Med and relied on him for special cuts of meat and a winning strategy for creating a feast.

Turning the page to July 3, 1966, I began to read the diary entries through 1983.

> *Page 2*
> Dinner for Charlesons, Seyberths, Tekla Culver, Beady Johnson, Dot Flemming, Gladdie, and the Proctors. Everyone cheered for the beef stew, wild rice from the Turk's Inn, Hayward, Wisconsin, leaf lettuce, glazed carrots, chocolate sponge cake, and fresh strawberries; invited

Millie Lasker. but she was visiting her sister in
Chetek.

While my diary discovery could have slipped into a sweet trip
down memory lane, I quickly recognized that it spoke of something
much larger than nostalgia. It highlighted our family's perception of
food, what it meant then, and how it continues to "flavor" our lives
today; how it delivers joy to both the cook and the guests. Thanks to
my mother (and, no doubt, Med), I have always believed that food
wields a mighty power for the comfort it brings to heart, body, and soul.

Though not a natural-born chef, Mom learned early in her
marriage that food functioned as a universal language. Ultimately, it
connected her to each of us and to countless others during times of
celebration as well as sorrow. In fact, her own sorrow following the
death of her first child awakened in her a whole new pleasure in good
food and heartfelt hospitality. Instead of shrinking in pain or locking
the door and pulling the shades to avoid another encounter with
sadness, she made a different choice: she learned how to cook. She also
grew to understand that infusing meals with loving-kindness was
powerful medicine—for her and for her guests.

Having read Deborah Kesten's book on food-related beliefs of
various wisdom traditions, I realized that our family and countless
friends had been treated to my mother's gift. She honored food through
thoughtful preparation and then offered it to all of us with depth and
sincerity. I even could imagine it being sacred, sanctified by her
warmth and affection.

When we appreciate food, as she did, we too contribute in an essential way to our well-being. The spiritual potential of food encompasses everything, from the soil that produces what we eat, to the thoughtful act of preparing and serving meals. Food, in the most profound ways, brings us into community with others to listen, smell, taste, and talk. No wonder my earlier description of our Outstanding in the Field dinner felt so powerful. Food tends to encourage intimacy and foster feelings of safety, even among strangers! It also sparks memories and invites storytelling. Whether enjoying a boisterous holiday dinner or a tiny driveway picnic with a few socially distanced neighbors, we reap the benefits of breaking bread together.

Though she probably never studied the religious and cultural nuances of food, I'm certain that my mother's inherent understanding of its value explained why she kept a food diary. Nowhere in its pages did I find notations about how many calories or grams of sugar, fat, or protein filled her "Ida May's Birthday Cake," or her crown roast of pork. Instead, she filled every line with lists of friends and relatives who came for dinner and stayed to play gin rummy or bridge. Couples and singles; widows and divorced; gay and straight; Republicans and Democrats; Jews and Christians—everyone was welcomed at her table.

Through the years, I have grown to appreciate her lifelong influence of food as a rich source of hospitality. For me, she freed food from the conflicts and confusion over endless weight-loss fads, eating disorders, cravings, addictions, and body-image fixations. She showed me what it meant to cook with intention for a wounded child or a friend recovering from chemotherapy. She understood that infusing meals with loving-kindness was, and is today, strong medicine. Imagine how much joy that gave her and everyone who came into her reach.

So, for Mom, doors closed in painful ways. Yet the rest of her world opened to a new day, once she clarified what she needed to help her feel whole again. Like most of us, her grief didn't get fixed or just disappear. It did, however, became a catalyst for self-discovery. She ultimately chose to befriend her personal gifts—to coexist with painful memories rather than be debilitated by them.

I spent the better part of that fall afternoon paging from month to month through the diary, making notes of fall and holiday recipes and lists of friends who might enjoy an autumn feast. And that's when I arrived at a late diary entry featuring my birthday.

March 27, 1983
Mary's B Day Party; favorite friends Veda, David, Wendy, Emma and Ralph, Bea and Sam, Oscar Sperstead. Med suggested a rolled eight-pound rib-eye roast (two hours and 20 minutes at 325 degrees), grapefruit and orange salad, mashed pots with dill and yogurt, baked asparagus, homemade bread, Isabel's German chocolate cake with ice cream. Isabel stopped in for dessert.

Rather than tipping me into a sentimental slump, this last entry launched me into the kitchen to investigate the possibilities. Maybe it was time to whip up a chicken pot pie, or, better yet, an Oktoberfest celebration to bring in the spirit of the harvest from my retiring vegetable garden. True, I wasn't harvesting much more than a few lingering tomatoes and a pot of herbs that had not yet frozen, but that was enough to get started. And then I came up with a list of good eaters. All I needed was the menu. Hence, the following entry into my own fledgling diary:

Late autumn, Labor Day has passed, Oktoberfest approaching:

Andra, Jen and Jon, Chris, Stephanie, Hal and Lynn, Vicki and David, Ethan and Hannah. Slow-cooked short ribs, fresh-herbed spaetzli, Grandma Gladdie's red cabbage, German potato salad, Black Forest cake with whipped cream.

Robust appetites required; lederhosen and dirndls optional.

Chapter 9
Maturity Points Us toward Acceptance

For everything there is a season and t time and a time for

every matter under heaven.

—Ecclesiastes 3:1

Irene, the daughter of neighborhood friends, called me recently to talk about her elderly father. A once-vital and intellectually curious man, he was now struggling with declining health. She described how he had faced a series of setbacks that often accompany aging—loss of friends, loss of professional standing, loss of energy. Then she asked me, "How many times have you heard an older adult say, 'It's really nice to be old'?"

I could not think of any. To the contrary, we are more likely to hear the opposite, including discouragement, dismay, and disbelief at the number of years that have passed. Yet like most kinds of loss that

61

we experience in our lives, aging frequently unleashes other setbacks. These could include having to leave one's home or give up hobbies and community activities—losses that cannot be assuaged with well-meaning platitudes.

We knew this family well and deeply admired her father. He was highly regarded and enjoyed a reputation as an honorable attorney who contributed generously to his community. So, I asked her tell me a story about a typical day in her life with him. I captured that story and believe it offers a study of aging toward acceptance and peace.

They sat at opposite ends of the kitchen table, father and daughter, comfortable with the long silences that yawned and stretched between them that morning. The previous week's unseasonably warm weather had been good for his health. Traditionally, these first weeks of April found them watching together for signs of the earth coming to life. A soft transition from winter to a season of kinder disposition helped him regain some of the stamina necessary to get through another year. For the next few months, they would be free of bone-chilling squalls of snow and sleet. No more plummeting thermometers. Though not yet balmy, winter had loosened its grip and given way to a new day. A pale thin sun bathed the early morning sky.

Migrating downy woodpeckers converged on a chunk of suet hanging from a linden tree. A few doves scuttled under the bird feeder, picking at leftover seeds. Fiddleheads poked cautiously through the thawing ground cover.

"He has always responded to the certainty of spring," said the daughter. "I think it helps him remember good things."

This day, he wore his flannel pajama bottoms and an undershirt. A shower of blood vessels fell across the paper-thin skin of his forearms. Years of using steroids to keep his emphysema at bay had taken a heavy toll, both on his moods and on his physical appearance. Nonetheless, this would be a good day.

She watched him methodically ingest an array of capsules and prepare to use an inhaler to relieve his labored breathing. He paused briefly between each dose of pills to observe, with obvious amusement, his dog, Cookie, in the backyard, poking among winter dry leaves in search of voles. Maybe all dogs recognize familiar scents that announced an arrival of a new season. Raising her head to the breeze, Cookie basked in the warming sun and sounds that rekindle life in the upper Midwest.

All living creatures respond to the earth's seasonal transformations. Hibernating and migrating patterns, social and working patterns—they all demonstrate the influence of our earth recreating herself. Research into northern winters has long suggested that people become more depressed during months when there are fewer hours of daylight. The seasons influence the way we work and live, what we wear, the foods we eat, and the homes we build. We respond in countless ways to the cycle of the seasons and the qualities of the earth.

Our interest in the earth is no accident or fleeting trend but one that accompanies us into old age. We have a vital need to be close to the earth and to all her expressions. It is critical that we learn to protect and preserve her precious resources and fragile beauty. She is vulnerable, as we are vulnerable. Even our vast resources of technology and science do not make us less vulnerable or less apt to get old and sick. We are born from the earth and nurtured by her, and we will ultimately return to her. Coming to peace with this truth is an essential task of aging.

Irene described her father as a man who embodied wisdom and courage, gained through years of living fully and well. For the better part of a century, he had enjoyed a fine adventure, as well as a brilliant law career. Both were filled with personal and intellectual accomplishments. He also enjoyed a hearty ability to laugh, especially at himself.

No way could his life be reduced to a simple exercise of growing up and growing old. Maturity such as his represented an inner growth toward wholeness. It brought to light a strength that transcended the past. This enabled him to live in the present and engage deeply in a world that includes suffering, sickness, and old age, with all its diminishments.

Contrary to what we might have learned, human maturity doesn't just happen. It requires the presence of certain assets, such as a community of friends, family, colleagues, and others who function as nurturers and censors of one another's values. A mature person like Irene's father has learned to consider his life experience through the eyes of his spiritual self. It's a quality that helps him not just to survive but to interpret the events that surround him as part of a larger, more meaningful whole. His clarity of vision influenced everything from the way he celebrated to the ways he found support in his pain and illness.

Listening to Irene's commentary on her father helped me understand what kind of grit it must have taken for him to move from vital, productive years through a difficult transition into retirement. He now faced the final leg of his journey into old age.

This morning felt to her like a last passage into a quieter and delicate time. No longer did her father engage in courtroom gymnastics or wade the Brule River with his fly rod and creel. Gone were the days when he scoured Bayfield County, flushing pheasant with his favorite hunting dog. He couldn't see so well anymore. He couldn't hear too well either. Some days, he felt just plain lousy and let everyone know it. Some days, he slept too much and groused about everything from the cost of groceries to the messy garage.

On other days, he pulled on his long underwear, rounded up Cookie, and drove to Chetek to buy homemade sausage from a farmer he had known for years. Another afternoon, he put in his hearing aid and spent a few hours conversing with his grandchildren. Or he rustled up a few remaining cohorts and set out for a lunch spot, where they regaled each another with exaggerated stories about Prohibition, deer hunting, and basement poker games.

In Irene's eyes, if ever there was a life worth living, it surely was her father's. On all fronts, professionally and personally, he challenged life, made friends with life, poked fun at life, and, finally, with fearless dignity, accepted aspects of life over which he had no control. Even then, as he stood face-to-face with the end of his life, he continued to savor its richness.

This was not a man who sought publicity or fame. He never needed to travel far or accumulate a larger worldly experience. In fact, he preferred to stay home. Surely he appreciated the success of his achievements, yet his real success lay in his ability to learn and to change when change was necessary. His accomplishments came in making substantial legal decisions and in his splendid sense of humor.

Never did he stop learning, Irene explained, and never did he give up a chance to move closer to becoming the person he was meant to be. Some days, that person had nothing bigger to do than ride his exercise bicycle on an imaginary trip to Bloomer.

Aging and illness invite us inward in search of things that won't fall to the ground or decay like last fall's leaves. It pulls us toward an interior spiritual light that will not fade. This inward journey of the human spirit is not just a goal or level of achievement that we work to attain. It is a faith-fueled process, ever moving, ever changing.

Like Irene's father, our spiritual lives arise from our human lives. They reflect the way we live and interpret the mystery that surrounds us. It includes the ways we maintain traditions, how we recover from loss, and how we find reconciliation with events and others. Our spiritual lives nurture our political and social behaviors, as well as the gifts we share with others. It includes our outlooks on our work and our attitudes about our time on earth. Our spiritual journeys cry out with a message of liberation. It's about unlearning fear and prejudice and freeing ourselves from restrictions of space, time, and matter.

Movement toward acceptance of life evolves from years of searching. It takes decades of self-discovery and new beginnings. Like Irene's father, we learn great truths over time and usually by looking backward at them. We need time and vision to order and shape our lives. We struggle to understand our experiences and the people around us. We attempt to make sense of ourselves and our less-than-manageable parts. We touch the chaos of our interior selves and realize that we may safely befriend them.

Maturity finally comes with the washing away of all that holds us back or impedes our healing and progress toward becoming our authentic selves. Maturity explores the possibilities. It touches our humanness with compassion. It wrestles with only the real things that obstruct our paths to a life of gratitude and joy. Maturity means celebrating the memory of our past and preserving the wisdom that the past gives to us today and to the new ordering of our lives. Finally, the acceptance that comes with maturity signals a breakthrough—that it releases us from our enclosures and teaches us how to love.

Chapter 10
Making Grace a Way of Life

Piglet noticed that even though he had a very
small heart, it could hold a rather large amount
of gratitude.

—A. A. Milne, *Winnie-the-Pooh*

The word *gratitude* finds its roots in the Latin word *gratia*, meaning grace, graciousness, or gratefulness, depending on context; sometimes it includes all three. Today, researchers continue to explore what gratitude means and how it works to improve one's sense of well-being. But what is it? An emotion? A virtue? A behavior? For centuries, religious leaders and philosophers have understood the virtues of gratitude. More recently, researchers in the field of positive psychology have learned a great deal about the biological roots of gratitude, including the benefits it delivers to those who practice it.

Our personal experience tells us that gratitude acknowledges thankfulness. Expressing gratitude helps us appreciate what we have received in life. It further helps us feel as if we have given something meaningful back to a person who has helped us. We could call it a feeling of gracious appreciation for goodness received from the hands of God, from another person, or from the world around us. Someone else might say that gratitude encompasses the simple blessings that come to us each day. Yet another would answer that expressing gratitude also strengthens relationships and functions as the social glue that helps us create and preserve relationships. In each case, most would agree that expressions of gratitude are important, powerful, and sometimes even life-changing.

Dr. Martin E. P. Seligman, a psychologist at the University of Pennsylvania, wanted to know more about gratitude and its role in mental health. So he tested the impact of several positive-psychology happiness interventions on 411 people. Each participant received an assignment to write and personally deliver a letter of gratitude to someone who had never been properly thanked for his or her kindness. The positive impact of writing and delivering these letters proved eye-opening. Among all the other happiness interventions he had tested, this one was the most successful, with a lasting impact of at least a month on the writers.[*]

---

[*] "In Praise of Gratitude," Harvard Medical Health Letter (updated June 5, 2019), https://www.health.harvard.edu/mind-and-mood/in-praise-of-gratitude.

Initially, the gratitude research struck me as a kind of smiley-face response to life, including life's problems. Some things just need more than a kind gesture, or so I thought. But once I received the same letter-writing assignment at a health-and-wellness conference, I saw the error of my assumption. The first gratitude letter I penned went to my daughter. It was hard to tell which one of us benefited the most, but the experience emboldened me to start sending random letters of appreciation. Off they went to retired college writing professors, favorite authors, and even a couple of prominent thought leaders and theologians who had inspired me over the years. The striking part about this exercise was that it made little difference to me if I heard from the letters' recipients. For all I knew, the letters could have gone to the wrong address. However, the mere process of contemplating what these individuals had given me left a memorable imprint on my own sense of well-being.

At one point, I drafted letter to a fellow we called "Small-Job Bob," a local handyman who could repair, repaint, or rebuild almost anything. Bob had helped in so many ways to transform my new home into my very own space. Even my pets felt grateful for Bob—he made an emergency run to my house early one morning to rescue my cat Tootsie, who got trapped under a kitchen cabinet. In his case, I personally read the letter to him while sitting on the bathroom counter as he painted the walls a lovely shade of aqua and hung an attractive new mirror. He was so surprised that he wordlessly snatched the letter from me and tucked it in his pocket. Sometimes, silence makes the clearest statement of appreciation.

This experience further convinced me that expressing gratitude through a letter positively affects both the writer and the recipient. The simple process is a potent one that seems to affirm that, overall, life is good and offers unexpected aspects that make it worth living. Soon after my letter-writing barrage, I stumbled upon a new level of shared gratitude. It had had nothing to do with dispatching a note.

It began with an invitation to speak at an event in my hometown of Eau Claire, Wisconsin. The presentation explored the difference between joy, happiness, and pleasure. It covered a range of fundamentals that contribute to and detract from authentic joy. We talked about everything from the power of listening, to our lives, to reviewing our beliefs, to releasing our grudges and disappointments and growing in resilience. The audience of about forty attentive listeners asked lots of questions and offered perceptive reflections. The dim lighting enabled me to show a few slides, though that made it difficult to see any faces.

Eventually, the gallery manager reminded me that closing time was approaching and asked how long we would be. I had planned to invite the group to wrap up our evening together by writing a gratitude letter, but time was running out. Instead, I explained the purpose and research surrounding the exercise and suggested that they try this when they got home. More questions and animated conversation followed. At some point during the discussion, a woman in the back row stood up and raised her hand. Though it was hard to see her in the darkened room, I assumed she had a question or comment for me, but she left her seat, walked the length of the room, and stood next to another woman who was sitting directly in front of me. The seated woman showed no sign of recognizing the other one. Then, the stranger said to her, "I want you to know that you changed my life."

The entire room appeared to take a deep breath. The speaker then shared a story of something that had happened years earlier.

"It took place in the Admissions Office at the University of Wisconsin," she began. "I had my heart set on entering college in the fall, and that morning, I was there to learn the results of my entrance exam. The exam had surprised me, as it was unlike anything I'd ever taken before, and no one had told me I should prepare for it. That became evident upon learning that I had failed the test and would not be accepted."

The seated woman appeared to be recalling this event, though she didn't say a word; she continued to listen.

"The whole thing was such a shock and so demoralizing," continued the standing woman. "All I wanted to do was run from that office and never come back. But you stopped me at the door. You asked me to come with you to another office, where you then explained how and why the preparation process mattered. You described how taking a practice exam would help me understand the kind of questions to expect. Then you told me where to make another appointment to retake the exam. I never even knew your name, but I have thought of that day so many times. Not only did you restore my self-confidence, but you pointed me in a new and rewarding direction."

By now the seated woman was fully engaged. She obviously remembered the incident but continued her silence, allowing the other woman to finish her story.

"So I did exactly as you suggested," she continued. "I prepared for and passed the entrance exam. Then I enrolled that fall and graduated three years later near the top of my class. At that point, I decided to study law and applied to Hamline law school in Saint Paul. That's where I earned my Juris Doctor degree, and I now have my own law firm, where we practice social justice law."

The seated woman simply smiled and said thank you. The rest of the room sat silently spellbound.

We are a world that constantly breaks down and analyzes component parts. We thrive on objective observation and tangible evidence. We measure and manage data, seeking proof and establishing metrics. Yet in our busyness and goal-setting, we sometimes miss the power of touching someone's heart, influencing a child, or even changing a life with a generous and sincere gesture.

How easy it is to spend our time and energy pursuing what we currently don't have. Gratitude reverses these priorities by helping us appreciate the people, places, and life experiences we already possess. It also unshackles us from toxic emotions. It's about finding goodness in the whole of life, rather than in specific goals or things. Living a life of gratitude means accepting its entirety as fundamentally good and meaningful. It implies gladness of spirit or a gladdening of the heart.

Chapter 11
Laughter—It's No Joke

Humour is, in fact, a prelude to faith; and laughter is the beginning of prayer.

—Reinhold Niebuhr

Years of research confirms that laughing does us good. Data collected by the Mayo Clinic says a hearty sense of humor might not cure all ailments or mitigate every setback and sorrow, but it can serve as a significant form of stress relief. A good laugh does more than lighten one's load, mentally. It induces physical changes in the body. Laughter can enhance one's intake of oxygen-rich air; stimulate the heart, lungs, and muscles; and increase endorphins released by the brain. Further, a wholehearted laugh activates and relieves our stress response, soothes tension, and stimulates circulation and muscle relaxation. And these are just the short-term effects.

Suggested long-term benefits are that laughter may improve the immune system, relieve pain, and make it easier to cope with difficult situations, such as chronic illness and depression. My personal experience tells me that laughter and humor bring us down to earth and make us less likely to take ourselves too seriously. Most people I've known with a hearty sense of humor strike me as more approachable and better connected to humility. I've also observed that humor is likely to influence a person's capacity for joy.[†]

Call it joyful or just plain silly, my father understood the anatomy of humor. I might have been ten years old when my dad, an upstanding circuit court judge, handed me a gift-wrapped copy of Damon Runyon's *Guys and Dolls*. While this might seem an odd choice of reading material for a ten-year-old girl, it suited me perfectly. Since Dad had been reading to me from this book, I had already fallen in love with the feckless, adorable gambler, Nathan Detroit. Runyon's outrageous characters made such an impression on me that Nicely Nicely Johnson and Harry the Horse appeared in my book *Never Say Neigh*, cowritten with my own horse. Writing the book probably stirred up more laughter and silliness for me than for readers. Even some of the scenes vaguely resembled *Guys and Dolls* capers.

In short, my father, the Judge, understood the meaning of *funny* and shared his gift with our family, early and often. A quintessential storyteller, he paid attention to details that others missed. For example, when my grandparents' elderly Norwegian housekeeper, Clara

---

[†] https://www.mayoclinic.org/healthy-lifestyle/stress-management/in-depth/stress-relief/art-20044456.

Christiansen, explained how her husband had died, nobody but the Judge heard her say the poor fellow died of "applestrokesy." This irregular version of the medical condition apoplexy soon found its way into the Farr humor lexicon. As for Clara, she remained a lifelong source of humor as an adopted member of our extended family.

Meanwhile, the humor business spread like poison ivy through our household. Stories became jewels to be intermittently exhumed and polished up for new audiences. Some family member was constantly delighting us with irreverent tales, like the deer-hunting lark at Camp Rum Dum in northern Wisconsin. This so-called deer camp served as a destination for faux hunters and geezers who pretended to track deer every fall. One example detailed a so-called hunting expedition that included the Judge and a couple of his retired chipmunk stalkers. The four oldsters made their way to Camp Rum Dum for one last hunting hurrah. To my knowledge, nobody ever bagged a deer, but they ate well and played lots of cribbage.

The tale goes like this: One night, an errant weasel found its way into the cabin. Nobody discovered it until after lights-out. The fearless hunters drifted off to sleep, and that's when the story took a wild turn. Awakened by a noise in the kitchen, they watched the weasel dive off the kitchen table, where it had been dining on apple pie. Not only did the weasel run for cover, but it made a couple of revolutions around the cabin and dived into old Ed Witzick's sleeping bag— alongside Ed. At that point, Ed's friend, retired sheriff Ray, clearly startled by the weasel invasion, discharged his service revolver inside the cabin. The rumpus that followed included Ed galloping out the door, barefoot, wearing only his long underwear. Of course, this story improved with years of embellishment.

Another favorite legend involved an incident in the Judge's courtroom. We were amazed to hear that a member of the Tarbox family was found guilty of pinching a few dairy goats from the neighbor's pasture. This courtroom appearance included a good deal of colorful testimony from numerous members of the Tarbox family. It also became public information at the end of the trial, when Grandma Tarbox slugged the district attorney with her purse. The ensuing rumpus took place in the courtroom after the Judge and his court reporter had retired to his chambers. The brawl managed to make a good story in the local newspaper.

And then there was Artie B. Sullivan, who piloted his new Cadillac into Mrs. Burrows's fish pond following a square dance at the local rod and gun club. Tales such as these set the tone for countless dinner conversations. My mother just rolled her eyes.

Somehow, I concluded, at about age eleven, that it was time for me to start writing humor or at least what struck my funny bone. My first book, *I Think My Brother Likes Me*, failed, due to what the editor called "inappropriate treatment" of our Labrador retriever, Sam. We loved Sam, and all we had done was hide him in the car trunk for a hasty ride to school for show-and-tell. It was a while before I submitted another manuscript to an uppity editor.

So here it is, fifty years later, and nothing has changed. My brother has picked up the storytelling mantle where the Judge left off. I've been known to blog and maintain a Twitter account for my horse and fellow author, Noah Vail. I've also appreciated my own experience in learning how humor offers yet another priceless value.

One Sunday morning in a senior living facility, I had agreed to substitute for a fellow chaplain who was unable to officiate the scheduled Sunday church service. It took place a short time after my ordination, and I looked forward to this new experience; I had every intention of doing sterling job. This involved planning a morning prayer liturgy, accompanied by a hope-filled homily. The facility's chapel was comfortable and bright, and a staff member selected several familiar hymns and accompanied the singers on a handsome Steinway piano.

When the day arrived, I took special care to dress accordingly, including a clerical collar, which we often did not wear in our hospital setting. In this case, it seemed appropriate to let people know who I was and why I had joined them. It was a lovely sunny morning, and the guests started to arrive early. The animated group included a man and woman who tottered to the first row in front of the podium where I stood. The woman was doing most of the chatting and seemed to be his guide.

After introducing myself and explaining why Father Phillips could not join them this morning, we began the service. The guests sang with gusto, and the pianist did a wonderful job. Frankly, I was feeling rather proficient, navigating this new experience. My homily appeared to meet expectations, though by this time, the gentleman accompanied by the chatty woman had fallen asleep. We finished with a final hymn, and I offered a blessing.

Suddenly, the woman poked the snoozing gentleman with her elbow, startling him awake, whereupon she pronounced at the top of her voice, "Wilbur, can you believe that these good people forgot to send us a minister today?" Wilbur simply smiled and nodded in agreement.

It was an illuminating moment. This dear fellow had enjoyed the service immensely. He had sung with gusto. He had chatted with his companion. He had enjoyed a little nap. By all accounts, he'd had a fine time. It just happened that he didn't notice the minister standing in front of him.

The coffee hour passed with plenty of sweets and amiable conversation. Staff members offered polite appreciation before making hasty retreats to their offices or workstations. It wasn't until I got to my car that I realized what a funny, albeit humbling, morning it had been. I laughed all the way home.

It's no coincidence that *humor* and *humble* come from the same Latin word, *humus*, meaning ground or earth. To be human is to be of the earth, to be an earthling. To be humble is to become aware of what we are made of—dust. Humor invites us to grow in humility. It takes us out of ourselves and reminds us of our capacity for pretense and preoccupation with our public images. We are simply earthlings of the earth. And some days, the earth has something to teach us.

One more amazingly silly story had just unfolded in front of me, and I became the joke. I'm convinced that this is what my father was trying to show us—that we all need to learn to laugh out loud at ourselves and at the situations in which we find ourselves, even if someone falls asleep during our sermon. Maybe that was the real humor lesson that the Judge was angling for. Let's not take ourselves too seriously.

Chapter 12
Thanksgiving Walk—Return to Your Senses

The poet Robert Frost often wrote about our earth's seasons. His poem "My November Guest" describes the quiet beauty of late fall. The poem also captures a mood set forth during the interlude between autumn and winter. It's a time when we start preparing for months of cold, snow, and indoor sanctuary. November, for those of us who live in the upper Midwest, calls up mixed emotions: the prospect of heavy winter boots and frostbite, countered by an invitation to enter a still space within our hearts and minds.

While all this might sound like hot chocolate in front of a cozy fire, autumn 2020 has delivered a very different world of illness, unrest, and fear. For me, it underscores the words of Dr. Martin Luther King Jr.: "We must accept finite disappointment, but never lose infinite hope." By choosing to turn away from finite disappointment, I believe we can trust this season of winter darkness to be a source of transformation and promise.

Each of our seasons speaks from its own mystery. Each reveals a message about life's passages and the inner flow of time. In October, the mood shifts toward closure, eventually leaving behind brilliant autumn colors and summer pastimes. The morning sun sleeps later. Sharp-shinned hawks and crows chase one another through the maple trees. Canada geese gather above nearby Dutch Lake to practice test flights before heading South. My vibrant garden behind the Methodist Church has given up its last bit of color and melted into subtle shades of brown. Soon, the remnants of squash and tomato plants will be hauled away to compost in preparation for spring planting. Early evening darkness drives us indoors and inspires quiet reflection.

Meanwhile, though autumn heralds the dying of a season, it does not mean the dying of inspiration or the end of growth. In truth, November highlights both the passing of summer and the beginning of our earth's renewal. It's about shifting gears toward our core. If renewal is the very nature of life, autumn promises to recharge all growing things in anticipation of the next leg of the journey.

A look at my own backyard proves this. The hydrangeas and lilacs have already set their buds in preparation to return for another spring. The truth of this—that renewal comprises the very nature of life—shapes my mood every fall morning, when my dog Winnie joins me for walk. It also reminds me of our annual Thanksgiving Day tradition, heading out into the dark for a frosty hike. My previous home in the city was perfectly located for meandering through a neighborhood of 1950s bungalows, statuesque churches, and Macalester College's empty campus. Naked oaks stood guard along the boulevards, braced against a sky that promised snow. Chipmunks scuttled through the dry leaves, packing acorns for the coming months. Norway pines framed an austere skyline and tranquil campus. The last remaining geese sailed overhead, announcing their exit from the cold to a more hospitable climate.

On one occasion, as we strolled through the streets and alleys, I remember stopping to observe the first glimmer of lamplight inside a stately Victorian home. The neighborhood was beginning to wake up. Watching households emerge from darkness filled me with a sense of closeness to those stirring inside. I imagined them shuffling about in their bathrobes, feeding the cat or unfolding the newspaper. Maybe sitting at the kitchen table with a hot cup of coffee. Some might have prayed, or worried, or simply read the editorial page. Hours from now, their homes might be overflowing with family and holiday guests. Or maybe it would be a day of restful contentment or even loneliness. It reminded me that while life after November offers us colder, darker landscapes, our desire for peace and contentment remains the same.

We are, in some ways, products of our earth's seasons. The fall calls us to reach into the depths of our lives and examine our courses. Or perhaps redirect them. We build fires in the fireplace and add blankets to the bed linens. We take more naps and read more books. We move indoors and enter the interior recesses of our homes and thoughts. It's a season of watchwords: Wait. Listen. Wait for snow.

Wait for cold. Wait for wisdom, clarity, direction. Wait for spring's reawakening.

Meanwhile, we do our waiting in a world that persists in doing and accomplishing, more than it considers the implications of its actions. Technology has become the scribe of our society, recording at warp speed our deeds, locations, and discoveries. René Descartes, a sixteenth-century French philosopher, often receives credit for creating our present worldview. It's a philosophy that has fostered tremendous growth of science and education. Cartesian thought, combined with the introduction of the printing press, brought the spread of ideas and literature throughout Europe. With the establishment of this way of observing the world, knowledge became information *about* things and people, rather than a personal encounter with life. Knowledge was gathered and recorded, one fact at a time. The journey from printed words to head-spinning technology and data collection had begun.

Before this, we lived in a sensuous world in which people relied on the ear and all the sense organs. Reality was experienced by sight, touch, smell, and taste. The oral story held a position of great importance to cultural health and history. A November walk into darkness could be trusted to reveal important truths. Though none of our senses disappeared with the introduction of science and technology, the world about which they tell us has become more suspect. If we can't provide hard evidence and the metrics to prove its value, it might not qualify as worthy or truthful. In today's world of battling truths, the soulful experience rates as questionable or simply wrong. Yet personal reflection and self-awareness are much more than gauzy time-wasters.

They're trustworthy sources of truth that can help heal our world. They tell us that how we care is as important as what we know. A walk in the dark on Thanksgiving morning shows us that we must never be ashamed of the heart and all its implications of forgiveness, gratitude, and loving-kindness.

Some say today's quest to recover ancient wisdom and healing traditions serves as a reaction to Descartes's world. Many of these traditions attempt to recover some of the vital acoustical senses within our life encounters. This matters because, despite its immeasurable value, Descartes's worldview defines life merely as what is material and observable. From where the dog and I walk on these frosty autumn mornings, his worldview defines life on very stingy terms.

We don't know when we will be touched by wisdom that emerges from an uncomplicated morning walk or a darkening winter sky. So in the months when the earth and her inhabitants settle into violet stillness, I will carefully observe this morning and know that hope is a worthy and realistic goal, no matter the state of our world or of our lives. Renewal is always possible, and life itself waits for us to stop, recharge, and let the light of hope lead us. Better yet, let us *be* a light of hope and return to our senses.

Chapter 13
Forgive More

Our goal is to create a beloved community, and this
will require a qualitative change in our souls as well as
a quantitative change in our lives.

—Dr. Martin Luther King Jr.

Who hasn't been deeply hurt by the actions or words of another? Maybe the injury stemmed from a critical parent or a trusted partner who engaged in an affair. You or someone you know might have suffered domestic abuse. Or the hurt could have begun with the onset of a life-changing illness. No matter the circumstance, deep wounds can open the door to anger, resentment, and depression.

Not long ago, I participated in a retreat that included presentations and small discussion circles that conversed about vulnerability, courage, shame, and forgiveness. Of the seventeen attendees, thirteen revealed, over the course of three days, that they had been sexually assaulted, one by her own brother. The group consisted of women, ages thirty-five to sixty-five. They connected well with one another and enjoyed plenty of spirited conversations about the topics, particularly the topic of forgiveness. In preparation for the final day, the moderator gave us an assignment. She asked that we each prepare a visual—a drawing, photograph or whatever we chose—to help describe where we found ourselves, spiritually and emotionally, at the end of the retreat. We had the evening to prepare.

The last day, when the final hour arrived, the moderator invited each of us to present our take-away summaries of the retreat topics and what insights we had gained about ourselves. The first sixteen presentations were upbeat and amusing, prompting hoots of laughter from the group. That was, until the last woman stood up to share her thoughts, the one who had admitted to being assaulted by her brother. She held a large piece of cardboard covered with rows of photos. Each photo documented something memorable from her childhood. They covered everything from birthday parties and Christmas trees with gifts beneath, to her favorite pony, her pet border collie, girlfriends, and picnics with her grandparents. After each detailed description of these happy events, she would add, "This was before my brother hurt me."

Her pain was palpable, and everyone felt it. This woman literally had stopped living her life after an unthinkable event took place in her own home.

"There is an enormous physical burden to being hurt and disappointed," says Karen Swartz, MD, director of the Mood Disorders

Adult Consultation Clinic at the Johns Hopkins Hospital.[‡] Chronic anger puts one into a flight-or-fight mode, resulting in numerous changes in heart rate, blood pressure, and immune response. Those changes increase the risk of depression, heart disease, and diabetes, among other conditions. Clinging to bitterness from such a wounding experience sets one up to pay dearly—physically, emotionally, and spiritually. It also closes the door to any prospect of joy.

We live in an imperfect world, and sometimes forgiveness looks and feels impossible. On the other hand, when we find that we can make peace with the reality of this imperfect world, we essentially forgive reality for being what it is. One could say we are agreeing to coexist with imperfection by not letting it consume us. That doesn't mean a hurtful act just disappears. And it does not excuse the harm done. What it does do is help to loosen its grip on the recipient of that harm. It frees one from the control of the person or event that has caused pain. In the case of the woman at the retreat, her wound was preventing her from attaining wholeness.

The act of forgiveness has many emotional, spiritual, and medical implications. It also means different things to different people. For example, forgiveness is central in various faith traditions and is non-negotiable in my own Christian tradition. It can foster a person's sense of self-acceptance as well as empathy, if she or he chooses to consider the goodness over the faults of another. One thing is certain:

[‡] Johns Hopkins Health, "Forgiveness: Your Health Depends on It," https://www.hopkinsmedicine.org/health/wellness-and-prevention/forgiveness-your-health-depends-on-it.

whether we lose a job, endure a bitter divorce, or face an act of violence, we constantly encounter unresolved conflict in need of forgiveness. The real surprise is how difficult it is to let go of resentment and thoughts of revenge. While there is no simple path to forgiveness, it is vital to one's health and happiness to find a way.

Genuine amends can clear the path to reconciliation. Yet it's possible that an injured party, such as the woman at the retreat, has no desire to make up with the author of her pain. In this case, she still can find forgiveness and experience a kind of release that helps free her from the connection to the distressing event. This process also can help her move forward through life, rather than remain stuck under it. Though not the same as reconciliation or trust, forgiveness makes these at least possible, provided one is genuinely sorry for causing the crisis. In any case, even this promising news does not make forgiveness an easy course. It's an individual one that requires commitment to a personalized plan of change. It's a practice that also benefits from the guidance of a health professional or spiritual mentor.

A very different aspect of forgiveness came to my attention this week. First it snowed. Let me rephrase that. This week between Christmas and the New Year, Minnesota hosted a genuine blizzard. It began with driving winds and pelting rain, followed by a foot of snow. Within hours, the outside temperatures had plummeted to subzero, making the roads virtually impassable.

No question, Minnesota enjoys a reputation for its challenging winters, but this first storm of the season occurred ten months into the COVID-19 pandemic, combined with months of bitter social upheaval.

Not only have communities throughout the world faced insurmountable loss and sickness, but most residents remain homebound, isolated, and getting on one another's nerves. Social violence and ugly political polarization have left wounds on entire cities and extended families. Words fail to describe the level of estrangement that has corroded so many relationships. So this is what I was thinking about while walking my Parson Russell terrier, Winnie, early on that morning after our first blizzard. How do we even begin to think about forgiveness and healing with our world in such a state?

Typically, a big storm sets off an assault of plows, Bobcats, pickups, and anything else that can move snow. That was not the case this holiday week. Sidewalks knee-deep in drifts offered a challenge for a small dog and his walking partner, dressed in ungainly rubber muck boots. So Winnie and I headed toward a nearby grocery store, hoping that a city plow had made a pass at their large parking lot. I was wrong. The lot looked like Lake Superior in white polar fleece. It was better suited for snowshoeing than dog walking. A couple of buried cars had likely spent the night there and were going to need a tow. Though it was barely daylight, a few older adults slogged through the drifts to take advantage of pandemic-safe sunrise shopping.

As Winnie and I approached the store, I noticed an elderly man stooped over an old-fashioned bicycle, not the fat-tired winter version. He stood next to the store entrance, pondering how to secure a full grocery bag to the handlebars. Dressed in a thick woolen coat and hat, he also wore a face mask emblazoned with Christmas trees. I estimated his age at about ninety years. As we approached him, the fellow greeted us cheerfully and complimented the dog's bright orange jacket. So we stopped to chat with him as he attempted to attach the bag. I noticed he wore a bandanna tied around his pant leg, presumably to keep his trousers out of the bike chain. Clearly, he had carefully planned this winter biking expedition.

Then he stood up and pulled a dog treat from his pocket and gave it to Winnie while we discussed the beauty of the snowfall. He seemed a little anxious to get on his bike, so we wished one another a happy New Year, and Winnie and I ducked around the corner of the building. The big question was, how in the world did he plan to make it through the parking lot without taking a spill—or worse? I decided to wait and watch nearby until he was either safely on his way or had given up and was ready to accept a ride. At this point, even getting on the bike posed a challenge for him. After a couple of false starts, he took off, wobbling through the parking lot and on to a busy street. I held my breath and watched as cars carefully motored around him. Finally, he disappeared down the street. Winnie and I headed home, where I jumped into my car and drove nearly a mile to an assisted living facility. Anticipating that this might have been his destination, I turned into the driveway and discovered his old bicycle standing next to the entrance.

This extraordinary encounter left me wondering who this man was. He certainly seemed competent and bright. What made him fearlessly take off on a bicycle through heavy snow and cold? What did he hope to achieve? With precious few details at my disposal, I decided to construct a picture in my mind of who he was and how this had happened. I envisioned him missing his deceased wife and being tired of visiting his children and grandchildren through his apartment window. If he belonged to a church, he probably had to attend via Zoom. He retired years ago, and several of his friends had become ill with COVID-19 or were otherwise unable to join him for a walk. He was tired of television news and angry politics. He had finished the last book in William Kent Krueger's Cork O'Connor series.

Then, he woke up this morning and said aloud, "This must change! I must change." He looked outside at the beautiful winter landscape and said, "By God, I've got life left in me, and I intend to start living it. Today. I'll begin with a bike ride to the grocery store, where I can wish a few strangers a happy New Year!"

The more I thought about it, the more my pretend narrative sounded like forgiveness—a choice made by an old man to shift from resentment to empathy and a new outlook on life. It felt like a healing response to a year stuck in illness and rage. Could this be a way to begin thinking and walking toward forgiveness. Might this path have the potential for healing our earth and all her guests? "By God, we have life to live together. And we have the gifts and grace to become a beloved community."

Chapter 14
Where Hope and Gratitude Meet

I said to the night

that stood at the gate of spring ascending,

"Give me a light

that I might tread safely

into the dark and through the unknown."

And a voice said in reply,

"Put your hand into the hand of the one who made you,

and your reward will be

blessed with more light,

courage,

and compassion,

far safer than the unknown."

A moment when God speaks

And we humans hear and are moved toward love.

When I asked him the meaning of *hope*, a wise friend told me, "Most people tend to associate hope with optimism. I find it more helpful to define the optimist as someone who says everything is going to be fine. The pessimist says everything will be awful. The hopeful person says, 'However things shall be, God can and will bring forth life.'"

This must be true, for there are many occasions on which we have no reason for optimism but every reason for hope.

One of those occasions took place in the month of January. The young parents in the emergency room where I worked as a chaplain watched without words as a team of physicians, pharmacists, respiratory therapists, nurses, and more labored over their baby boy. Hoping against hope, the man and woman gripped each other's hands and prayed together for a miracle that would revive their son. Born just a few weeks earlier, Stephen was diagnosed at birth with hemophilia, though, by all accounts, he was doing well.

They had been surprised at their good fortune of an unplanned pregnancy, and both Stephen's parents and his older siblings were thrilled at the baby boy's arrival. The instant he emerged from his mother's womb, he became the cooing center of his family's adoration. His ecstatic parents clucked attentively over his every move, keeping a watchful eye on all aspects of his care.

This morning, however, something had gone terribly wrong. Somewhere between a family rejoicing at breakfast over their exquisite son and the father's drive home from a visit with relatives, Stephen died. He produced not a sound, not a seizure, not a hint of warning. He simply stopped breathing. More shocking, his father did not discover the catastrophe until he parked the car in the garage and reached into the back seat to lift Stephen from his infant seat. In an instant, the mystery of love that created him and prepared a place for him was about to come to terms with letting him go.

After what seemed an interminable hour, the emergency room physician in charge of resuscitation efforts stopped and looked helplessly into the parents' faces. It was hardly necessary for her to speak, as everyone had known—or at least had suspected—the outcome before the painstaking attempt to revive Stephen even began. The rest of the trauma team backed away from the baby, paralyzed by agony and disbelief. It was sudden infant death syndrome. It was over.

What happened next, however, would transform this devastating loss into a life-changing experience of a very different nature. Stephen's parents, crushed beyond description, turned to the group and thanked each person in the room for her or his valiant effort to save Stephen's life. The couple then thanked each other for the life they had shared for many years. They thanked their family physician and the clinic nurses who had provided Stephen's ongoing care. They even thanked the paramedics who raced to their home and toiled in vain to breathe life back into Stephen.

Finally, though tearful and shaky, Stephen's father gently wrapped his son in a clean receiving blanket, lifted the baby upward toward the blinding trauma room lights, thanked God for sharing Stephen with him and his family, and then baptized the lifeless child. It was a gesture of gratitude that brought the normally bustling emergency department to a speechless standstill. The tables had turned. A family who had lost more than words could say had extended a healing hand and heartfelt gesture of gratitude to the professional caregivers.

"There is no tragedy, nor is there any kind of loss, through which life cannot come forward," said Stephen's father, several weeks later. "Sometimes we simply have no control, and all we can do is try to go on living our lives with integrity. Stephen's death was outside of our control, but we trust that life can come from it. We know grace can be in it."

Several months later, Stephen's physician was to offer the address at a hospital memorial service held for all the families whose children had died in the past year. Before an auditorium full of pensive faces, he spoke about mercy and gratitude and how important a role both played in the practice of medicine. He then simply thanked the members of the audience. He thanked them for teaching him about children and for allowing him to care for their children. He thanked them for sharing their wisdom about loss with him. Then he told a story about the death of his father.

What a long and difficult path the two had walked together, through relationship challenges and his father's treatment for debilitating heart disease. The doctor described the gratitude he felt for his father's life and how the two of them had made a point of expressing their appreciation for the blessings of a shared life. He talked about compassion and spoke with simplicity of heart about how it felt to have no cure to offer. Eventually, he told the story of his father's last hours, the bathing and gently turning him and changing of his bedclothes. He described massaging his father's feet and hands, all the tender care that prevails when clinical practice becomes moot. At the end, each man said thank you to the other and to the silence. And they said goodbye.

After witnessing both of those events, I realized that there are some things in life we can take into our hands and hold up to the light or put under a microscope for a clearer understanding. We can sift through a handful of pebbles or inspect a beautiful piece of silk. We can perceive the magnificence of a masterful painting; we can observe the petals of a rose. But there are other matters that we cannot grasp with our hands or eyes but only with our hearts. These extend beyond our reach and our comprehension. They carry us past the conscious world of familiar scenery and sounds into the silent world of the unknown. Some would describe these experiences as encounters with mystery, the revelation of something hidden. In the case of the family and the physician, the mystery originates in their posture of gratitude for all of life—life blessed and life broken. Father to son. Son to father. Theirs was an unbroken circle of mercy and gratitude, a connection of the heart that begins in life and remains in death.

Stephen died in the month of January. January receives its name from Janus, the god of thresholds. Janus is often pictured with two faces. One face looks backward in memory, and the other face searches the horizon of the future. Janus is also the patron of doorways. The month that bears his name marks the season of endings and beginnings, as in the beginning of a new year. It is the time of inventories. January is the month of resuming old routines after the holidays and starting new ones that sustain us through the rest of the winter.

The ability to assume a posture of gratitude does not make crossing the January threshold and beginning anew any less difficult or painful. Beginnings and endings never come easily. Adjusting life plans and reshaping lost dreams takes tremendous courage. To adapt their visions and their directions is a challenge that stood before Stephen's family, before their physicians, and before most of us much of the time. These are the things that sometimes make us wonder if we should stretch out our hands to welcome another day or turn over and pull the blanket over our heads. Shall we hide from life, or shall we embrace it? Can we find a reason to hope?

Most of us experience growth and understanding of our journeys in fleeting glimpses, rather than in dramatic turning points. Truth unfolds slowly more often than it appears in great flashes of light. Its pattern remains hidden beneath the routine events of the day. Even if hope tells us our lives have a different direction and a destiny, it's only in gifted moments that we gain enough perspective to see this mosaic of meaning.

An ancient Orphic hymn proclaims that the night is the birth of all things. January takes us out into the bitter cold, yet for Stephen's parents and for his doctor, the darkness of January was not a night of despair only but a night of watching for the light of January. They came to realize that in life, as in death, we are truly linked together by a most fragile thread. Creation and compassion give birth to this delicate link. Gratitude and mercy sustain it.

Chapter 15
The Healing Power of Empathy

No one listens, they tell me, and so I listen. And I tell
them what they have just told me, and I sit in silence,
listening to them, letting them grieve. "Julian you are
wise," they say. "You have been gifted with
understanding." And all I did was listen, for I believe
full surely that God's spirit is in us all.

—Julian of Norwich, fifteenth-century English mystic

Hospitals have provided me with a professional and vocational home
since my junior year of high school. Though the work has transitioned
from volunteer to medical illustrator to communications and hospital
chaplaincy, my opinion of nurses has never wavered. *Hero, champion,*
and *compassionate advocate* come to mind when speaking of nurses.
This is particularly true today, when they have spent a year caring for

overwhelming numbers of patients, families, and colleagues. It also explains why, early in my chaplaincy experience, I developed a bond with the Minnesota Parish Nurses Association.

This association reflects the historic values of medieval Europe's nursing role in hospital care. In fact, nursing care was originally provided by religious communities, including nuns and monks. During the late 700s and early 800s, Emperor Charlemagne decreed that deteriorating hospitals be restored, and each should be attached to a cathedral or a monastery. *Hotel-Dieu,* an old French term for hospital, literally meant "hostel of God."

This small piece of history also set the stage for a conversation I initiated with a local parish nurse association. Parish nursing combines ministry with the art and science of nursing, ever mindful of the strong relationship between faith and health. Parish nurses are registered nurses who complete additional study in health promotion, illness prevention, and support for families during life's difficult circumstances. My work included many opportunities to partner with these nurses. I sincerely value their commitment to care of both mind and body, particularly when circumstances involve grave news.

It's hard to start a conversation with someone who is suffering. Harder still is the worry that we won't know how to open a conversation or what to say once we get there. Our concern about uttering the wrong thing and our discomfort over inserting ourselves into someone's troubles can be overwhelming. This awkwardness might even cause us to turn away from their distress and go about our own business. Yet, in my experience, we rarely make a mistake when we let someone know that we care. And our expression of concern doesn't need to be fraught with anxiety. To care about someone's well-being and to act with compassion can infuse a remarkable amount of healing energy into any sorrowful situation. Everyone is enriched when we see and respond to each other with empathy and compassion.

This truth became the core of our conversation that evening. The parish nurse role and mine required that we bring to a joyful or sometimes difficult situation, a sense of the holy. This included a promise of God's presence and a concern for the human spirit, a spirit that offers the potential for healing. Our role also included a responsibility to honor and care for our own spiritual needs, a task that can get lost or ignored when caring for others.

The evening began with my challenge to them. "We must remember and apply each of this evening's objectives—particularly that of empathy—to ourselves and to those for whom we care."

As we progressed through the evening, discussing our tasks as patient and family advocates, we realized that each of us had our own stories to tell and losses to visit. We came to our jobs bearing our own histories and life situations. And we could not ignore this. While it was important to check our agendas at the door, it was not possible or even wise, to check our histories at the door when we visited a patient, a friend, or a family member experiencing a loss. Truthfully, these are the stories that provided a source of wisdom for each of us, whether we work in a hospital or classroom or belong to a book club. Our stories provide a pool of experience we can draw from when we face our own or another's loss.

We each possess stories that can deliver wisdom—just consider the year 2020. Not only has the world undergone a crushing series of events, but the cost of these events likely will continue to emerge. The implications from them could reach far beyond lost lives, jobs, and relationships. I believe they have touched our souls at the deepest level and probably will continue to shape our lives in ways we might not yet understand. It's vital to articulate this story of where we were and how it has touched us. How do we establish order and meaning to our lives? How do we support one another when we encounter a confusing turn in the road? Where are the guideposts? In what can we trust?

For example, a nurse that evening told me about the death of her second parent. Though she and her siblings had mourned the passing of her father several years earlier, it was the death of her mother that set off a chain of events and additional sorrows. She described a loss of holiday traditions; the family home, where she and her siblings had grown up; and the many familiar contents of that home. The safe shelter they still called home was no longer available for making family memories. The second parent's death also resulted in the loss of contact with old family friends. She described feeling like an orphan at age fifty.

So, a single traumatic event or serious illness often plays out in additional costs for which we might not be prepared. A true healing process, whether from a death or a broken world, involves a thoughtful examination of the entire loss before we can integrate it and move forward.

My evening with the parish nurse association brought about a deeper respect and acceptance of our individual and collective losses. We realized how this impacted our professional lives. We experienced a more meaningful appreciation of self-compassion and empathy. Additionally, beyond our own roles, we were reminded that virtually everyone works and interacts with people who have been marginalized or injured in some manner—by illness, old age, color, isolation, and disability. Each of these holds a story of loss. I truly believe that when we articulate our own stories and listen to our own hearts and wisdom, we prepare ourselves to move forward with a renewed capacity to grow in empathy and bring more light into the world.

I think we underestimate our ability to help heal—ourselves and others. We don't have to be a nurse or a chaplain to show up and listen. We can grow in empathy and self-compassion by becoming more adept at perceiving emotions and by finding ways to encourage and support one another. We can let go of judgment. We can step outside our own experiences and attend to another's. We can claim a reason to hope.

In the heart of every person is a longing for justice and a desire to make sense of life. We do not find it difficult to discover meaning in life when we are experiencing good days. When we feel secure and certain, we find life quite acceptable. When there is bread on our tables and health in our families, we can toast the wine of life with glad hearts. But what about the painful times? How can we make sense of these? How do we become healed? Why do the innocent suffer? Why do good people have to face personal tragedy?

As my evening with the parish nurses came to a close, I realized that pastoral ministry, whether delivered in a church, a parish nurse program, a fire department, a classroom, a nursing home, or a hospital is a gift we each can bring to the day. It entails little more than a willingness to be present with one another. It doesn't require doing things to people, but it does promise to shine hope on another's path. We might not fix or manipulate or diagnose, but we can agree to walk one another home.

Chapter 16
Walking the Dog

The new dawn blooms as we free it

For there is always light,

if only we're brave enough to see it

If only we're brave enough to be it

—Amanda Gorman, National Youth Poet Laureate

"The Hill We Climb"

It was mid-April when it dawned on me. I hardly knew one day from the next. Monday felt like Thursday. Weekends blended somewhere in the middle. Interrupted routines, stymied employment, and sporadic haircuts wreaked havoc with anything resembling a schedule. Weekly highlights consisted of following pandemic reports and staking out Costco sales of Cabernet Sauvignon. It seemed as if all rhythm and logic had vanished—everything, that is, except for one thing: walking the dog. My Parson Russell terrier, Winnie, and her chum, Tootsie, the barn cat, have done their best to keep me in sync with their demands for food and exercise.

Every morning, Tootsie sounded the reveille call for breakfast at 6:30. An hour later, a friendly neighbor met me by my mailbox with her little dog, Lilly. The four of us then soldiered off into the dawn, wondering when we would be able to visit our relatives and exchange our winter boots for hiking shoes. Some mornings, we're greeted by sub-zero temperatures and icy walkways. More than once, I had to carry a protesting Winnie out the door. She's a clever dog who understands the joy of napping indoors by a sunny window. Sometimes, we were tempted to stay home but did not. Even in the dead of Minnesota winter, the walks delivered a certain cadence to the day, a dose of normalcy in the middle of disarray.

Eventually, longer days and earlier sunrises moved us toward spring. This also made our dog walks more inviting. And that wasn't the only change. My friend Marian and I began to appreciate the absence of morning television news. We started to see the wisdom of getting out of the house, no matter what the weather served up. Walking away from that constant drumbeat of polarized politics and public health projections offered us welcome relief. We felt downright liberated, marching around in the dark, enjoying heavenly silence.

That treasured silence ultimately shifted to something new. Sounds and sights of spring began to appear on those tranquil morning hikes. A shimmering sun rose in orderly silence. A chorus of frogs broke into song as we came near their half-frozen pond on the Dakota

Trail. Even thirty degrees and driving wet snow couldn't deter cardinals from calling to each other. Social media diatribes could not prevent them from mating and raising their broods. Red-twig dogwood awakened in the ditches and along the lakeside. A pileated woodpecker busied itself pounding on an oak tree that had fallen near the path. Such a miracle that just a month ago we had endured fifteen degrees below zero. Walking required ice cleats attached to the bottoms of our boots.

These miraculous new changes delivered us yet another emotion—hope. Marian and I, and probably our dogs, felt the cold darkness quietly lift from a new kind of morning. Even Winnie and Lilly behaved as if something promising waited for them on the path ahead. It could have been nothing more than a few good smells, but they trotted along with fresh enthusiasm. Busy gray squirrels skittered among the sumac bushes. A young fox sprinted across the path, followed by two feral cats. It was hard to miss the evidence of spring emerging.

Though I have often spoken and written about the healing treasures of the earth's seasons, I couldn't remember having been so moved by these changes. Maybe it was the predictability of spring that helped us feel some growing sense of order. Or it could have been the crabapple tree, full of red-winged blackbirds calling *conk-la-ree*. I do know that it felt as if we were watching a choreographed arrival of a new season in time.

So on that chilly April day, we headed out once more to test the meaning of our early-morning walks—except that on that morning, we took careful note of each budding sign that proved we had made it through a harsh winter. Every squirrel hoarding acorns. Every feral cat surveying its territory. Every crow calling out a morning report to its companions.

It struck me that maybe … just maybe this miracle of new life that delivered my neighbor and me from despair also was showing us what healing and joyful renewal could look like.

Now, if only we humans can pay attention.

Chapter 17
Friendship: It's about Wasting Time Wisely—Together

Saint Francis of Assisi lived in Italy during the late twelfth and early thirteenth centuries. Born of great wealth, he left that life to found the Catholic Church's Franciscan order. He was not a highly educated man, and he did not write a systematic theology summarizing the doctrines of religion. Instead, he became known for his generosity to the poor and his willingness to minister to lepers. Franciscan theology is also called a theology of the environment. Indeed, Pope Gregory IX pronounced Saint Francis the patron saint of the environment *and* its animals.

Francis allegedly preached to even the birds. He believed that God is good. Therefore, creation, because it is a primary revelation of God, must also be good. Stated another way, creation for Francis provided a visible sign of an invisible God. It is a sacrament or sacred. Francis's theology included a reverence for each aspect of creation, from the smallest creature to Brother Sun; from Sister Moon and the stars to Brother Wind and all the weather. His "Canticle of the Creatures" sums up Francis's love of the natural world in a single verse:

> Be praised, my Lord, through Sister Mother Earth,
> Who sustains us and guides us,
> And produces diverse fruits with colored flowers
> and herbs.

Saint Francis believed that each element of nature reflected a unique aspect of the divine.

Even today, many Christian traditions celebrate the Feast of Saint Francis, held on October 4. This typically includes a blessing of the animals, including dogs, cats, gerbils, parrots, and then some. I've even had the opportunity of blessing a few willing cows.

Somewhere in her Episcopalian upbringing, my mother must have experienced a close encounter with Franciscan theology. Her genuine love of the environment showed in every tree and perennial garden she planted; in every bird feeder she hung or bat cave she discovered. She also loved a star-filled night sky and could identify constellations that we never studied in school. Cumulous clouds, thunderstorms, hedgerows sheltering meadowlarks and foxes—she never missed an opportunity to share these treasures with anyone who cared to listen. We did and still do, as my writing suggests.

All of this serves as a backdrop for a starless night in early spring, when my good friend Emma and I drove off into the predawn darkness to count migrating sandhill cranes. We were taking part in an annual event sponsored by the National Audubon Society. The outing involved groups of enthusiastic bird-watchers setting out for various marshes and wildlife sanctuaries throughout Minnesota and Wisconsin. The object was to listen for calls that signaled the return of these splendid birds. Then, after several chilly hours of waiting and counting, volunteers would gather, tally up their numbers, and hope that the sandhill crane was safe for another year.

This grand adventure required hitting the road by 3:00 a.m., as official bird counting began before daybreak. Upon arriving at our site, a guide would instruct us to hike into the woods and find a place where we could sit quietly. Once settled in an observation site, we would tune into the blackness until approximately 7:30 a.m., or whenever the frozen ground forced us to take cover. Five of us drove together that morning. Over the country roads we bumped, drinking coffee out of paper cups while quibbling over directions to an unmarked swamp near Fairchild, Wisconsin. It was an adventure that demanded a good base layer of long underwear and a flashlight with new batteries.

Once we arrived at our counting destination, our little group hiked another mile down a fire lane. This meant carrying an array of paper, pencils, blankets, and boat cushions on which to park ourselves. Loaded like packhorses, we groped through brush and staggered over fallen logs and through soggy ditches before finally arriving at our appointed stations.

Emma and I settled on some reasonably dry ground, while the others parked their belongings a short distance away. There we sat, absorbing the earthy fragrance of fallen oaks covered in lichen. In our effort to keep warm, we huddled under an old bedspread, chortling about everything unrelated to bird counting. The rest of our party cast chastising glances our way, clearly irritated by our irreverence for the occasion.

Properly chastened, we shifted our focus to a bag of doughnuts. At least it cut the conversation to a minimum. Then something happened that suggested we were in for a bigger event than bird counting. Somewhere between our mindless chatter and the doughnut bag, silence gave way to sound. It came from the swamp. It also prompted some serious shivering on my part as we huddled in the dark.

"What could it be?" squeaked Emma.

Night sounds. Wind whispering. Mysterious thuds and rustling leaves. Then, an eerie overture of sandhill guard calls, followed by unison cries from the illusive birds. One mate called to another. Their inelegant symphony rang through the trees. It sounded like a creation of other-worldly music sung from a foggy stage. The score then shifted to more melodious sounds, including something resembling a pitch pipe. It all blended into a ghostly sound that I would not soon forget.

Eventually, the cranes' songs quieted, and the softening glow of dawn began to reach skyward. But the ghostly entertainment was not over yet. A nighthawk took flight directly over our heads. Seconds later, a murder of crows descended upon the unsuspecting hawk. We could only stare into the fog and wonder what the outcome might have been. The entire swamp seemed to awaken at once. Wrapped in songs and screeches of emerging daybreak, we waited.

Once we recovered from the outbreak of unfamiliar birdsong, we began to grasp the meaning of what had happened. The promising sounds of awakening creation were ringing all around us. Undisturbed by careless use of herbicides and human technology, the woods had come alive before our eyes. In the east, an amber band of dawn spilled across the sky. Its light glinted off prisms of ice clinging to the marsh grasses. Without a sound, the sun suddenly rose like a fiery ember.

In the rolling hills and woods of western Wisconsin, this kind of morning landscape still waits for us to listen and watch. Growing older, I've come to understand this was more than a sketch of dawn or a pleasant outing with an old friend. My mother had already shown me how to appreciate summer days, tracking morel mushrooms and purple vetch. With a bucket of water and a *Peterson* bird guide, we spent hours driving through the hills and along the Mississippi River. We immersed ourselves in the kind of natural beauty that invites a different way of seeing, an experience of insight.

Our vision of life, as well as our happiness, is shaped by our surroundings. This includes our natural surroundings. Even as a child, I awakened early, eager to take a road trip designed to help me fall in love with the land. Today, that earth and sky of my childhood remain with me. They affect everything from my theology to my vision of the future.

We each carry these kinds of recollections, as memories and metaphors. They shape our language and our understanding of our life journeys. What I've learned is that the meaning of our days lies behind the ordinary. It speaks in quiet, earthy tones, not as high drama. These powerful images have always seasoned my writing and call to inspire others. They also serve as a source of great joy.

A spiritual experience, such as the one we encountered in that Wisconsin marsh, is a moment when God speaks, and we humans hear and are moved toward freedom. Sometimes this experience can be as simple as counting the cry of sandhill cranes returning to the Wisconsin wetlands.

Chapter 18
Finding a Source of Renewal and Refreshment

I find hope in the darkest of days and focus in the brightness. I do not judge the universe.

—Dalai Lama

Wish. Yearn. Long for. What do hope and renewal mean in today's world? We hope to stay well and safe. It's possible that we hope to find a job or return to the job we temporarily left or lost. We yearn to renew our connections with friends and relatives. We long for a sense of refreshment and a decent night's sleep. All these make perfect sense, though they felt somehow deficient on the day I visited a friend in Pennsylvania.

My friend had arranged a speaking engagement for me. The event took place at Christ Church, an Episcopal church in the Old City neighborhood of Philadelphia. Founded in 1695 as a Church of England parish, it played an integral role in the founding of the Protestant Episcopal Church in the United States. It also likely played a role in delivering hope to immigrants, many whose relatives had died in a deadly smallpox epidemic. Then, in 1793, came yellow fever; then scarlet fever in 1858. The list has gone on, until we now find ourselves amid another global health catastrophe, still wondering about that illusive promise of hope in the face of grueling times.

My audience that day consisted of educated and sophisticate older adults, including members of Christ Church, plus a few guests. We enjoyed a spirited conversation and questions that one might expect from an informed, affluent crowd. That was, until a young man stood up and waved my way with a comment that startled everyone.

"I'm homeless," he announced simply, "and my friends and colleagues on the street are homeless. When they ask me questions about hope, I don't know what to say to them. Since I'm part of a street ministry, I'm wondering if you can help me find a way or the words to make hope real for them."

Nobody was prepared for such a comment, though the group quickly became immersed in a sincere and supportive conversation. I believe the young man left that day somewhat encouraged with all the thoughtful observations and ideas that were offered. On the other hand, I have since spent hours exploring an authentic and applicable meaning of hope. How do we make it more than a platitude? How do we make it real and honest? How do we apply it to our current point in history? Our country? Our world? Our planet? How do we walk toward the future with faith and a realistic expectation of hope?

Noted Franciscan theologian Father Richard Rohr says, "The theological virtue of hope is the patient and trustful willingness to live without closure, without resolution, and still be content and even happy because our satisfaction is now at another level and our source is beyond ourselves."

The truth of this comes with a serious challenge. Willingness to patiently live without closure is a tough assignment in a culture such as ours. We are doers and fixers. We plan, build, repair, and measure the results of our work. Anything involving such a level of ambiguity, loose ends, or lack of resolution feels like failure.

So how do we hope in a broken world? I know one thing: we cannot wait for the future to come to us. We must create the future. We also might need to rethink the meaning of hope. On a personal level, I have chosen to invest in a few small and ordinary ways to maintain hope during a time when one could easily lose hope. These little "projects" have a common thread—refreshment and renewal that fosters hope.

Plant a garden.

This summer I signed up for a community garden bed provided by a nearby Methodist church. Though I've always enjoyed gardening, this has become a truly restorative experience. Snow and frost finally released their grip on our Minnesota landscape. The earth began to warm. Seeds sprouted, and frozen perennials miraculously emerged. Lilies of the valley forced their way through the thawing dirt. And lilacs bloomed profusely. I collected my vegetable garden seeds—peas, beans, and summer squash. Five tomato plants went into their sturdy cages. It was a springtime renewal of the highest order. A pleasure we can count on whether we are stuck cleaning the garage or planting ghost peppers.

Cook with friends.

We know that preparing food with intention creates a life-affirming and renewable connection with others. This has been especially true when most of the world's population has been locked down at home, separated from social activities. Though I'm no gourmet cook, I do understand that preparing and sharing food with others is very special. I've also learned that serving it on paper plates in the driveway to a handful of masked guests is just as special. Tater Tot hot dish tastes as good in the driveway as any fillet served in a fine-dining establishment.

This tiny entertaining practice turned out to be a neighborhood success. Soon, complete strangers were leaving invitations on our doors and contributing wine and food to the menus. Old church cookbooks and grandma recipes produced everything from lemon soufflé to lima bean salad. Often, small groups remained in their driveways, while others socialized from the middle of the street as they moseyed past, sipping their cold drinks and wishing everyone well. Not only did I host my own driveway birthday party, but four guests and two dogs joined me for Christmas in the garage, with doors open, lap blankets on every chair, and an outside temperature hovering at twenty degrees.

Consider birding.

My brother and I could tell a purple finch from a redpoll by age ten. Setting out birdfeeders and bluebird houses became a spring ritual at our house. We still put out bluebird houses in the spring and search for the best seed to lure doves and migrations of pine grosbeaks. To cement our commitment to birds, my mother gave us copies of Rachel Carson's *Silent Spring*. She made it clear, early and often, that birds and the environment provided the pulse of the world.

Today, when friends and I walk around Lake Minnetonka, we often see as many as six eagles diving and skirmishing with one another. Even a local osprey and its mate have entertained us with shrieks from atop a nearby cell tower. Each sighting reminds me that these remarkable birds are the hosts, and we are the guests on this earth. It also reminds me that feeding and observing birds yields a simple pastime that delivers real satisfaction.

Search for humor in all the odd places.

Humor tends to deliver strong medicine to the most difficult situations. It reminds us to loosen up and consider a different perspective. Humor, during a year that sometimes felt like solitary confinement, turned up in some unique and unexpected places. Take, for example, washing groceries before putting them away. That piece of pandemic advice struck me as debatable the minute I heard it. Nonetheless, it also yielded my first and last opportunity to shampoo an onion.

Meanwhile, Zoom gatherings, though necessary and helpful,

also invite comedy. From online church featuring Zoom-bombing pets, to first-timers unwittingly showing up in their nightgowns, it can feel like watching *Saturday Night Live*. Speaking of Zoom-bombing pets, both my dog and cat adore Zoom. These same pets also furnish nighttime entertainment. For example, one late night, my cat discovered a wayward field mouse that had made its way to my office. By the time I got out of bed and discovered the cause of the excitement, the mouse had taken a dive under a cabinet. The noise alerted the Parson Russell that raced to the scene. Suddenly, the mouse dashed from under the cabinet straight into the mouth of the Parson Russell. Perplexed, though uninjured, the tiny rodent bit the dog, who squealed and wisely spit it out.

Next, the mouse made a run toward the cat, which made a run for cover. In the end, the mouse circled around the room and headed for me. This turn of events caught me by surprise—so much so that I spontaneously reached out like a rookie center fielder and caught the little critter. It was a quick trip down the steps and out the front door in my pajamas before depositing the tiny invader in a pot of geraniums. The neighbors could only watch and wonder. If I ever doubted the value of nighttime acrobatics as humor, I've become a believer.

Chapter 19
Consider Joyful Awareness—the Power of Yes

To offer no resistance to life is to be in a state of grace,
ease, and lightness. This state is then no longer
dependent upon things being in a certain way, good or
bad.

— Eckhart Tolle

I'm convinced that few of us choose to change much. Instead, we tend to resist or simply forge ahead through an array of worn-out habits and ideas until all else fails. This truth came to my attention when it became clear that I had been resisting for a long time. Maybe it began as early as grade school when I skipped piano lessons in favor of riding my horse. Or stashed a pair of jeans in my locker so that I could change out of a skirt the minute I arrived at school.

More recently, my penchant for resistance has taken on new character. For example, why bother querying a publisher with that children's manuscript stashed in my desk drawer? Then there have been invitations to speak or teach. My answer usually veers toward no. Public speaking just stirs up needless anxiety. The word in question here is *no*. For reasons I don't fully understand, no has become easier to say than yes. No, I don't care to go to that restaurant. It's too loud, and we can't hear one another. No, I've had enough technology tutoring to exhaust Best Buy's Geek Squad. And no, please don't ask me to take an online intentional blogging course with a bunch of teenagers. (Admittedly, I did sign up for that and loved it.)

Others started to notice. Then, one day a colleague called to see how things were going in the work-at-home mode. It was a Friday and, after a few minutes catching up, she asked ever-so-politely, "So, what are you up to this weekend? Or do you plan to stay home and make clothes for the cat?" I was out of excuses.

True, my work life had changed significantly in recent years. Retired friends now spent summer at the lake and winter in warmer places. Social activity had waned a bit. Yet it should not come as a surprise that our plans frequently change direction over time. Jobs change. Relationships change, sometimes through our own doing and sometimes resulting from adversity. Sometimes it's simply the evolution of time and aging that produces changes. In each case, examining and adapting to our new reality helps pave the way back to saying yes.

The truth is, when we practice saying yes, we discover that it's good for friendships. It also broadens the possibilities for fun and opens doors to new adventures. Yes can even spark up a dull day and move us forward with resilience rather than resistance. Life opens lots more doors when we say yes. And that includes lots more opportunities for joy. The proof of this theory comes from a longtime family friend named Joan.

We have known Joan for years. My brother and I spent countless hours in her home as kids, largely because it offered great entertainment. The possibilities for fun were limitless. This included a generous mix of birthday parties on the front porch, model airplane building, and electric trains. Pet chameleons and cockatiels held court in Joan's dining room, especially during celebrations. She typically hosted holiday parties for friends, neighbors, and a cluster of local clergy. On one occasion, I watched her prize cockatiel make a three-point landing in a punch bowl. Rather than make a fuss, Joan simply plucked the bird from the punch, dashed to the kitchen, and rinsed it in a sink full of dishwater. She then collected a few feathers from the punch bowl and whisked it back to the dining room table.

Joan was the kind of person who would accept an invitation to do something exciting and new, then rush off to learn how to do it. She once took a European trip with her daughters and returned home with two Bernese mountain dogs, a plan to develop a breeding program, and a Volkswagen bus. The dog-breeding program stuck, and the bus provided future puppy transportation.

All these escapades explain why we were so saddened when Joan's husband, an Episcopalian bishop, retired, and the family moved to a southern Wisconsin farm. Frankly, the farm as a retirement destination surprised everyone. To my knowledge, no family member had any acquaintance with agriculture beyond a patch of asparagus growing their backyard.

Based on Joan's history as a city dweller, imagine my surprise when, a couple of years later, I drove into her farmyard and met a flock of geese serving as her security detail. Hissing and flapping, they ran at my car window as if I were on a Homeland Security watch list. Much to my relief, Joan rushed out of the house, waving a broom. She assured me it was safe if I stayed close to her. The geese finally gave in and waddled off to a nearby compost pile, all the while casting insults our way. It was then Joan introduced me to her five-year-old granddaughter, Christine, who had been taking in the goose escapade from the back steps. Christine marched past the grumbling gaggle and proceeded to lead the way on our farm tour.

When we reached our first stop, Christine climbed to the top of a rock pile and began sorting her collection of quartz and agates. Occasionally, she tossed a small stone into the pond below, prompting more cursing from the geese. Two Bernese mountain dogs joined in, loping about on the mountain of stones left over from last spring's pond dredging. Their chorus of barks rained down on Christine as she sorted her collection. The dogs careened in and out of the water, retrieving branches and wrestling with one another. Joan tried, with little success, to manage them. She finally convinced her granddaughter to come down and join us for a hike along the river. With that, Christine turned a somersault in the mud and skipped off, with the dogs barking behind her. Joan obviously encouraged this kind of merrymaking.

The driveway to her home offered the first clues to Joan's sense of fun. A sign next to the mailbox identified the farm as the Shepherd's Patch, a reference to her late husband, the Most Reverend William. A tilting flagpole served as a centerpiece for an array of toys, including a child's-size telescope for observing celestial events. The front porch, festooned with dog dishes and croquet mallets, also served as a stage for puppet shows. Two abandoned church pews leaned against the garage.

Christine then led us to our next stop, the barn. A welcome hex sign hung above the barn door. This inviting form of Pennsylvania Dutch folk art featured a heart surrounded by red tulips. Just inside the door we met two Cotswold rams named Willie Billie and Billy Willie, more reminders of the dear departed bishop. Behind the barn, a couple of dozen startled ewes swung their heads up as the dogs galloped through their pen, dragging a carcass.

Joan's toolshed, full of wire and stakes, stood behind a dead pickup truck that listed gently over its front tires. A faded sign nailed to the shed marked the property as a licensed game farm. Joan hatched pheasants in cooperation with the Wisconsin Department of Natural Resources. Her partnership with the DNR also hatched a pond-dredging project. This eventually became home to hundreds of small trout. It also created a spa for the dogs. No wonder her grandchildren sobbed bitterly when their parents retrieved them from this hotbed of entertainment.

Joan's wardrobe transitioned throughout the day, from barn to garden to marketing apparel. That morning she wore a lemon-yellow T-shirt and blue knit pants. She donned a baseball cap with an orange bird's-beak visor. Her rubber Muck boots added a fashion statement; plus, they provided some protection against irritable geese. Naysayers might have called Joan eccentric. Her grandchildren beheld her as a grown-up Peter Pan. She loved to watch them explore the natural world and encouraged them to taste something new. That explained the grocery bag filled with asparagus that Christine collected. The two of them planned to prepare it for dinner.

The sights and sounds of the Shepherd's Patch reflected Joan's unfettered tribute to life's simplest joys. Yet behind all this fun stood a woman who possessed character strengths and virtues that achieved a greater purpose than her own personal goals. Persistence, faith, and an inclination to say yes to adventure defined her life of many colors.

She was a terrible driver, famous for backing through garage doors and ferrying lambs in the back seat of her car. A woman with more than a few opinions, her deafening bellow could send a brave soul scampering for cover—or, more likely, for dinner. The house was a jumble of books and projects, including a large loom for anyone brave enough to tackle a weaving assignment.

She loved to travel. On one road trip, her daughters and I carried her in her bathing suit and plunked her in a Colorado hot spring. That same trip we gave her a tour of the Brass Ass Casino, where she tested the slots and won seven hundred dollars. After sipping a "winners" drink called Naked on the Beach, she gave the money to her daughter to start an inner-city youth computer program in a Boston library.

An avid reader, Joan's nightstand sagged under the weight of books, from the history of Ireland to Wensleydale cheese making. Each day, she operated with a full schedule, interrupted only by an occasional nap. Her spirit of discovery fed her sense of whimsy. In her words, "the fun is in the doing."

Watching Joan with Christine that morning, I saw a woman who had experienced her own sorrows. Her husband had died, and she lived alone, navigating health problems that might have crushed most people. Yet she continued to live in the present, saying yes to whatever life handed her on that day. Christine and her other grandchildren invited her to be with them here and now. Their uninhibited expressions of affection and enthusiasm pulled her into the moment. She simply celebrated life where she found it. She had a strong community of family and friends and a focal point somewhere outside of herself.

The family farm produced one more opportunity for Joan to try new things. It gave her a place to explore a new world of agriculture and share it with her family. Initially, she knew nothing about sheep, or carding wool, or operating a loom. Yet we were observing a beautiful flock and two handsome rams. I also doubt that she had ever dialed up the Department of Natural Resources for help. And behold, they showed up to rehabilitate a trout stream. She just seemed to know that saying yes was wondrously empowering.

Afterword

This is a wonderful day. I've never seen this one before.

—Maya Angelou

Hope constitutes a vital spiritual element in joy. Hope provides purpose, direction, and a reason for being. It's an attitude toward life, rather than an occasional feeling we turn to when we reach the end of our human limitations. Hope is a disposition that says the future is an open one, and we can dare to believe that it holds integrity. I have witnessed and personally discovered how hope engages our capacity to see ourselves in a larger landscape. This is a landscape in which we can transcend any situation or life chapter.

Yet we live in a culture that reminds us we are what we do. We are important if we do something important. We are intelligent if we do something intelligent or valuable if we do something of value. In short, individual achievements and successes are often viewed as synonymous with joy. Though dazzling accomplishments deliver plenty of satisfaction, they do not ensure sustainable peace or happiness. Ultimately, contentment comes from more than the high points or remarkable successes. It also immerges from our struggles and our willingness to be transformed. This kind of transformation entails discovering important truths about ourselves. It also could lead to resetting our beliefs and reviewing our relationships with the world around us.

The stories and individuals highlighted in this book suggest that human growth toward well-being can happen in an instant or can take years of learning, and unlearning. And it's never too late to start. Maybe it begins with a loss or an unexpected reversal. Or maybe we are facing the prospect of retirement, followed by a diminished professional identity. Important life changes such as these often provoke a kind of mourning. However, they also can point us toward deeper self-discovery and fresh beginnings. We learn new truths about ourselves. We uncover ignored talents and interests. We see more clearly that which brings us renewal and refreshment. The irony of this is that we often learn it by looking backward at where we've been.

So, wisdom does not necessarily come with the high points. Sometimes it requires the cleansing of all that holds us back or impedes our growth. Maturity explores the possibilities. It touches our humanness with empathy and compassion—for ourselves and for others. It wrestles with the real things that obstruct our way to wholeness. Maturity means examining the memories of our past and preserving the wisdom that it gives to today. Finally, spiritual wholeness signals a breakthrough. This breakthrough can release us from our enclosures and teach us what truly matters.

Through the years, I have listened to countless families and friends worry out loud about a future they cannot see. I too have wrung my hands over unseen and improbable events, as if my exercise in fretfulness might somehow stave off future disaster. I too have awakened in a fit of midnight insanity, convinced that I would never find another job or would be forced to spend my retirement years playing solitaire on my phone. But I also know that when I get caught up in this kind of cynicism, I forget to fully live the life that I am already in.

A fellow chaplain once said to me, "There is a freeway to doubt and fear and a footpath to peace and joy." Like my friend Joan, the eccentric sheepherder who invited her grandchildren to stargaze at midnight, I must stop and remember. When we nourish our faith in life's goodness, we become more willing to coexist with the full spectrum of its gifts and burdens.

About the Author

Mary Farr, a longtime pediatric and adult hospital chaplain has devoted years to exploring the worlds of hope, healing and humor. She infuses these qualities into her writing and teaching, from her award winning *Never Say Neigh*, to her current foray into the true meaning of joy. Her capacity to light up audiences with laughter and delight inspires kindness and concern for one and all.

Mary has published five books, including the critically acclaimed *If I Could Mend Your Heart; The Heart of Health*; Never Say Neigh; and *The Promise in Plan B*. She has inspired a variety of audiences including: the Hazelden Betty Ford Foundation, The Chautauqua Institution, CaringBridge, and the Minnesota Network of Hospice and Palliative Care.

A graduate of the University of Wisconsin, Mary completed divinity studies in the Episcopal Diocese of Eau Claire, Wisconsin where she was ordained to the permanent diaconate. She received a Masters of Theology from Saint Catherine University, Saint Paul, Minnesota and currently serves in pastoral ministry at St. Martin's By The Lake Episcopal Church, in Minnetonka Beach, Minnesota.

CPSIA information can be obtained
at www.ICGtesting.com
Printed in the USA
LVHW021739300323
743053LV00003B/511